# ESPAÑOL 2000

NIVEL ELEMENTAL

## GLOSARIO MULTILINGÜE

ESPAÑOL - ALEMÁN - INGLÉS - FRANCÉS

Nieves García Fernández
Jesús Sánchez Lobato

SOCIEDAD GENERAL ESPAÑOLA DE LIBRERÍA, S. A.

Primera edición en 1994
Quinta edición en el 2000

Produce: SGEL - Educación
 Avda. Valdelaparra, 29 - 28108 ALCOBENDAS (MADRID)

© Jesús Sánchez Lobato y Nieves García Fernández, 1994
© Sociedad General Española de Librería, S. A., 1994
 Avda. Valdelaparra, 29 - 28108 ALCOBENDAS (MADRID)

ISBN: 84-7143-499-7
Depósito Legal: M. 35.410 2000
Impreso en España - Printed in Spain

Composición e impresión: NUEVA IMPRENTA, S. A.
Encuadernación: EUROPA, S. A. L.

## A

| UNIDAD | ESPAÑOL | ALEMÁN | INGLÉS | FRANCÉS |
|---|---|---|---|---|
| 6 | a | um | to | a/en |
| 14 | abajo | unten | under | dessous |
| 1 | abogado, el | Rechtsanwalt, der | lawyer | l'avocat |
| 23 | abrazo, el | Umarmung, die | embrace | l'accolade |
| 5 | abrigo, el | Mantel, der | (over) coat | le manteau |
| 6 | abril | April, der | April | avril |
| 9 | abrir | öffnen | to open | ouvrir |
| 5 | abuelo, el | Großvater, der | grandfather | le grand-père |
| 16 | aburrido | langweilig | bored; boring | qui s'ennuie |
| 16 | aburrir(se) | (sich) langweiligen | to get/be bored | s'ennuyer |
| 21 | acabar de | et. soeben getan haben | have + just + p.p. | venir de |
| 13 | acabarse | aus sein; zu Ende gehen | to finish | se terminer |
| 16 | accidente, el | Unfall, der | accident | l'accident |
| 6 | aceituna, la | Olive, die | olive | l'olive |
|  | acentuar | betonen | to accent/to stress | accentuer |
| 7 | acera, la | Gehsteig, der | pavement | le trottoir |
| 20 | acero, el | Stahl, der | steel | l'acier |
| 7 | acertar | das Richtige treffen | to guess right | trouver |
| 1 | acierto, el | richtige Antwort, die | right answer | la solution |
| 8 | aconsejar | jmdm. raten | to advise | conseiller |
| 7 | acordar | verinbaren | to agree upon | se mettre d'accord |
| 10 | acordarse de | sich erinnern an | to remember | se rappeler |
| 7 | acostar(se) | ins Bett bringen/gehen | to go to bed | se coucher |
| 16 | acto, en el | sofort, auf der Stelle | immediately; on the spot | sur le coup |
| 20 | actor, el | Schauspieler, der | actor | l'acteur |
| 15 | actriz, la | Schauspielerin, die | actress | l'actrice |

| UNIDAD | ESPAÑOL | ALEMÁN | INGLÉS | FRANCÉS |
|---|---|---|---|---|
| 22 | actuar | handeln | to act | agir |
| 17 | acueducto, el | Aquädukt, der | aquaduct | l'aqueduc |
| 15 | acuerdo, el | Übereinstimmung, die | agreement | l'accord |
| 23 | adelante | vorwärts | besides; moreover | en avant; plus loin |
| 11 | además | außerdem | too; as well (as) | en plus |
| 9 | a diario | jeden Tag; täglich | daily; everyday | journellement; tous les jours |
| 1 | ¡adiós! | Auf Wiedersehen! | goodbye! | au revoir! |
| 12 | ¿a dónde? | wohin? | where to? | où? |
| 21 | adosado, el | Reihenhaus, das | terrace house | la maison rangée |
| 14 | aduana, la | Zoll, der | customs | la douane |
| 9 | advertir de | warnen vor | to warn | avertir |
| 12 | aeropuerto, el | Flughafen, der | airport | l'aéroport |
| 22 | afabilidad, la | Freundlichkeit, die | affability | affabilité |
| 9 | afeitar(se) | (sich) rasieren | to shave | se raser |
| 2 | africano | afrikanisch; Afrikaner, der | African | Africain |
| 22 | agencia de viajes, la | Reisebüro, das | travel agency | l'agence de voyages |
| 6 | agosto | August, der | August | Août |
| 13 | agotado | ausverkauft | sold out | vendu/epuisé |
| 12 | agoamiento, el | Erschöpfung, die | exhaustion | l'épuisement |
| 4 | agradable | gemütlich | pleasant | agréable |
| 23 | agradar | gefallen | to please | plaire |
| 23 | agrado, el | Gefallen, das | pleasure | plaisir |
| 3 | agua, el | Wasser, das | water | l'eau |
| 18 | aguantar | aushalten | to put up with | supporter |
| 3 | ahí | da; dort | there | là-bas |
| 4 | ahora | jetzt | now | maintenant |
| 11 | ahora mismo | gleich; sofort | right now | tout de suite |
| 14 | ahorrar | sparen | to save | épargner |
| 22 | aire acondicionado, el | Klimaanlage, die | air conditioning | l'air conditionné |
| 16 | ajetreado | anstrengend | busy | mouvementé |
| 3 | alcalde, el | Bürgermeistewr, der | mayor | le maire |
| 23 | alcanzar | crrcichcn | to reach | rattraper, atteindre |
| 17 | alcázar, el | Burg; Festigung, die | fortress | le château fort |
| 12 | alcohol, el | Alkohol, der | alcohol | l'alcool |
| 23 | alegrar(se) | (sich) freuen | to be glad | (se) réjouir |
| 4 | alegre | fröhlich | cheerful | gai |
| 22 | alegría, la | Freude, die | happiness | la joie |
| 2 | alemán | deutsch; Deutsche, der | German | Allemand |
| 4 | alfombra, la | Teppich, der | carpet | le tapis |
| 11 | algo | etwas | something; anything? | quelque chose |
| 11 | alguien | jemand | someone; anyone? | quelqu'un |
| 11 | algún | (irgend) ein | some, any? | quelque |

| UNIDAD | ESPAÑOL | ALEMÁN | INGLÉS | FRANCÉS |
|---|---|---|---|---|
| 7 | al lado (de) | nebenan; neben | next to | à côté de |
| 2 | alma, el | Seele, die | soul | l'âme |
| 13 | almacén, el | Kaufhaus, das | warehouse | le magasin; l'entrepôt |
| 20 | almorzar | zu Mittag essen | to have lunch | déjeuner |
| 14 | almuerzo, el | Mittagessen, das | lunch | le déjeuner |
| 12 | a lo largo de | entlang | along | au long de |
| 19 | a lo mejor | vielleicht | perhaps | peut-être |
| 19 | al parecer | anscheinend | it seems that… | apparemment |
| 7 | alquilar | (ver) mieten | to rent/to let | louer |
| 5 | alquiler, el | Miete, die | rent | la location |
| 12 | alrededor de | um… herum | around | alentour |
| 14 | altavoz, el | Lautsprecher, de | loudspeaker | le haut-parleur |
| 2 | alto | groß; hoch | tall, high | grand; haut |
| 5 | alumno, el | Schüler, der | pupil, student | l'élève |
| 3 | allí | da; dort | there | là-bas |
| 2 | amable | freundlich | kind | aimable |
| 14 | amanecer | tagen | to dawn/to break | se lever (le jour) |
| 13 | amargo | bitter | bitter | amer |
| 5 | amarillo | gelb | yellow | jaune |
| 16 | ambulancia, la | Krankenwagen, der | ambulance | l'ambulance |
| 9 | a menudo | oft | often | souvent |
| 2 | americano | amerikanisch; Amerikaner, der | American | américain |
| 1 | amigo, el | Freund, der | friend | l'ami |
| 21 | amueblar | möblieren | to furnish | meubler |
| 17 | andar | gehen | to walk | marcher |
| 19 | anillo, el | Ring, der | ring | l'anneau |
| 20 | animación, la | Beleben, das | liveliness | l'animation |
| 4 | anímico | seelisch | mental; psychic | animique |
| 6 | aniversario, el | Jubiläum, das | anniversary | l'anniversaire |
| 16 | anoche | gestern abend; nacht | last night | hier soir |
| 19 | anochecer | dämmern | to get dark | tomber (la nuit) |
| 16 | anteayer | vorgestern | the day before yesterday | avant-hier |
| 18 | anterior | früher; vorhergehend | previous; preceding | antérieur |
| 14 | antes | früher | before | avant |
| 3 | antiguo | alt | old | ancien |
| 2 | antipático | unsympathisch | unfriendly | antipathique |
| 17 | anuncio, el | Anzeige, die | advertisement | l'annonce |
| 18 | añadir | hinzufügen | to add | ajouter |
| 6 | año, el | Jahr, das | year | l'année |
| 12 | apagar | ausmachen | turn off; switch off | éteindre |
| 11 | aparato, el | Apparat, der | apparatus | l'appareil |
| 7 | aparcar | parken | to park | garer |
| 13 | aparecer | erscheinen | to appear | apparaître |
| 5 | apartamento, el | Appartement, das | flat; apartment | l'appartement |

| UNIDAD | ESPAÑOL | ALEMÁN | INGLÉS | FRANCÉS |
|---|---|---|---|---|
| 23 | a partir de | von .... an | starting (from) | à partir de |
| 12 | apellido, el | Familienname, der | surname | le nom de famille |
| 9 | apenas | kaum | hardly | à peine |
| 11 | apetecer | möchten; Lust haben | like; feel like | désirer |
| 20 | aplaudir | applaudiren; Beifall klatschen | to applaud; to clap | applaudir |
| 13 | aplicado | fleißig | diligent | appliqué |
| 23 | apoyo, el | Hilfe; Unterstützung, die | support | l'appui |
| 8 | aprender | lernen | to learn | apprendre |
| 11 | aprobar | bestehen | to approve; to pass | réussir |
| 19 | aproximadamente | circa; etwa; ungefähr | approximately | approximativement |
| 3 | aquel | der da/dort | that | ce...-lá |
| 3 | aquí | hier | here | ici |
| 17 | árabe | arabisch; Araber, der | Arab | l'arabe |
| 5 | árbol, el | Baum, der | tree | l'arbre |
| 2 | argentino | argentinisch; Argentinier, der | Argentine; Argentinian | Argentin |
| 4 | armario, el | Schrank, der | cupboard | l'armoire |
| 1 | arquitecto, el | Architekt, der | architect | l'architecte |
| 10 | arreglar | aufräumen; einrichten | to arrange; to organize | arranger; réparer |
| 11 | arte, el | Kunst, die | Art | l'art |
| 20 | artesanía, la | Handwerkkunst, die | craftsmanship | l'artisanat |
| 13 | asa, el | Henkel, der | handle | l'anse |
| 17 | asamblea, la | Versammlung, die | assembly | l'assemblée |
| 19 | asegurar | versichern | to assure | assurer |
| 18 | asfixiado | erstickt | asphyxiated; suffocated | asphyxié |
| 9 | así | so | so/like this | ainsi; comme cela |
| 2 | asiático | asiatisch; Asiat, der | Asian | asiatique |
| 11 | asiento, el | Platz; Sitz, der | seat | le siège |
| 14 | aspirina, la | Aspirin, das | aspirin | l'aspirine |
| 11 | asunto, el | Sache, die | issue; matter | l'affaire |
| 14 | atención, la | Achtung, die | attention | l'attention |
| 23 | atender | aufpassen; beachten; zuhören | to attend to; to pay attention to; to зcrvc | s'occcuper de; servir; recevoir; зatisfaire |
| 23 | atento | aufmerksam | attentive; observant | attentif |
| 21 | aterrizar | landen | to land | atterrir |
| 21 | ático, el | Dachgeschoß, das; | attic | l'attique; dernier étage |
| 14 | atleta, el/la | Athlet, der /-in, die | athlete | l'athlète |
| 10 | atmosférico | atmosphärisch | atmospheric | atmosphèrique |
| 19 | atrapar | verhaften | to catch; to trap | attraper; décrocher |
| 7 | atravesar | überqueren | to go across/over | traverser |
| 20 | atropellar | überfahren | to run over | renverser |
| 7 | aula, el | Hörsaal, der; Klassenzimmer, das | classroom | la salle de classe |

| UNIDAD | ESPAÑOL | ALEMÁN | INGLÉS | FRANCÉS |
|---|---|---|---|---|
| 7 | aún | noch | still; yet | encore |
| 10 | aunque | obwohl | although; though | bien que |
| 13 | auricular, el | Kopfhörer, der | headphone | l'auriculaire |
| 2 | australiano | australisch; Austrialer, der | Australian | Australien |
| 2 | austriaco | österreichisch; Österreicher, der | Austrian | Autrichien |
| 3 | autobús, el | Bus, der | bus | l'autobus |
| 22 | autocar, el | Reisebus, der | coach | le car |
| 17 | automóvil, el | Auto, das; | car | l'automobile |
| 4 | autonomía, la | Autonomie, die | autonomy | l'autonomie |
| 16 | autopista, la | Autobahn, die | motorway | l'autoroute |
| 17 | autor, el | Autor, der | author | l' auteur |
| 5 | autoritario | autoritär | authoritarian | autoritaire |
| 6 | a veces | manchmal | sometimes | parfois |
| 16 | aventura, la | Abenteuer, das | adventure | l'aventure |
| 14 | avería, la | Panne, die | breakdown | la panne |
| 17 | averiar(se) | eine Panne haben | to get damaged | tomber en panne |
| 11 | avión, el | Flugzeug, das | plane | l'avion |
| 17 | avisar | benachrichtigen; rufen | to call; to notify | appeler |
| 16 | ayer | gestern | yesterday | hier |
| 9 | ayuda, la | Hilfe, die | help | l' aide |
| 7 | ayudar | helfen | to help | aider |
| 3 | ayuntamiento, el | Rathaus, das | townhall | la mairie |
| 1 | azafata, la | Stewardeß, die | stewardess | Hôtesse |
| 4 | azul | blau | blue | bleu |

## B

| UNIDAD | ESPAÑOL | ALEMÁN | INGLÉS | FRANCÉS |
|---|---|---|---|---|
| 9 | bailar | tanzen | to dance | danser |
| 15 | bajar(se) | hinuntergehen | to go down; to get off | descendre |
| 2 | bajo | klein | low | bas |
| 13 | balcón, el | Balkon, der | balcony | le balcón |
| 3 | bambú, el | Bambus, der | bamboo | le Bambou |
| 3 | banco, el | Bank, die | bank | la banque |
| 9 | bañar(se) | baden; sich baden | to bathe; to bath | (se) baigner |
| 4 | baño, el | Bad, das | bath(room) | le bain |
| 2 | barato | billig | cheap | bon marché |
| 19 | barco, el | Schiff, das | ship | le bateau |
| 3 | bar, el | Kneipe; Gaststätte, die | bar | le bar |
| 5 | barrio, el | Stadtviertel, das | quarter; district | le quartier |
| 14 | báscula, la | Waage, die | scales | la bascule |
| 3 | bastante | ziemlich | enough | assez |
| 17 | batalla, la | Schlacht, die | battle | la bataille |
| 6 | bebé, el | Baby, das | baby | le bébé |
| 8 | beber | trinken | to drink | boire |
| 11 | bebida, la | Getränk, das | drink | la boisson |
| 23 | beca, la | Stipendium, das | grant; scholarship | la bourse |
| 2 | belga | belgisch; Belgier, der | Belgian | Belge |
| 17 | bello | schön | beautiful | beau |
| 17 | beso, el | Kuß, der | kiss | le baiser |
| 17 | biblia, la | Bibel, die | Bible | la bible |
| 5 | biblioteca, la | Bibliothek, die | library | la bibliotèque |
| 4 | bicicleta, la | Fahrrad, das | bicycle | la bicyclète |
| 4 | bien | gut | good | bien |
| 23 | bien, el | Gute, das | good | le bien |

| UNIDAD | ESPAÑOL | ALEMÁN | INGLÉS | FRANCÉS |
|---|---|---|---|---|
| 6 | billete, el | Fahrkarte, die | ticket | le billet |
| 6 | bisiesto | Schaltjahr, das | leap year | bissextile |
| 5 | blanco | weiß | white | blanc |
| 5 | blusa, la | Bluse, die | blouse | la blouse |
| 14 | boca del metro, la | U-Bahnstation, die | underground station | la bouche de métro |
| 14 | bocacalle, la | Querstraße, die | intersection, side board | l'entrée d'une rue |
| 6 | bocadillo, el | belegtes Brötchen | sandwich | le sandwich |
| 6 | boda, la | Hochzeit, die | wedding | le mariage |
| 22 | bodega, la | Weinkeller, der | cellar | la cave |
| 2 | boliviano | bolivianisch; Bolivianer, der | Bolivian | Bolivien |
| 6 | bolsa, la | Tüte, die | bag | le sac |
| 5 | bolso, el | Tasche, die | bag; purse | le sac à main |
| 17 | bomba, la | Bombe, die | bomb | la bombe |
| 20 | bombero, el | Feuerwehrmann, der | fireman | le pompier |
| 13 | bombilla, la | Birne, die | bulb | l'ampoule |
| 3 | bonito | schön | beautiful | joli |
| 23 | borrar | abwischen | to rub out; to erase | raturer; effacer |
| 12 | bota, la | Stiefel, der | boot | la botte |
| 4 | botella, la | Flasche, die | bottle | la bouteille |
| 2 | brasileño | brasilianisch; Brasilianer, der | Brazilian | Brésilien |
| 17 | brevemente | kurz | briefly | brièvement |
| 19 | broma, la | Scherz; Spaß, der | joke | la farce; la blague |
| 1 | buenas tardes | guten Tag; guten Abend | Good afternoon; Good evening | bonjour; bonsoir |
| 1 | bueno | gut | good | bon |
| 1 | buenos días | guten Morgen; guten Tag | Good morning | bonjour |
| 12 | bufanda, la | Halstuch, das | scarf | le cache-nez; l'écharpe |
| 21 | buhardilla, la | Dachkammer; Mansarde, die | attic; garret | la mansarde |
| 18 | buscar | suchen | to look for | chercher |

## C

| UNIDAD | ESPAÑOL | ALEMÁN | INGLÉS | FRANCÉS |
|---|---|---|---|---|
| 19 | caballo, el | Pferd, das | horse | le cheval |
| 17 | caber | Platz haben | to fit | tenir; entrer; rentrer |
| 12 | cabeza, la | Kopf, der | head | la tête |
| 17 | cada | jeder | each; every | chaque |
| 10 | caer(se) | (herunter) fallen | to fall (down) | tomber |
| 3 | café, el | Café, das; Kaffee, der | coffee | le café |
| 6 | café cortado, el | Kaffee mit wenig Milch | cup of coffee with a drop of milk | le café avec un petit peu du lait |
| 6 | café solo, el | schwarzer Kaffee | black coffee | le café noir |
| 3 | cafetería, la | Cafeteria, die; Café, das | cafeteria | le café |
| 17 | caja, la | Kiste, die | box | la boîte |
| 17 | caja de cambios, la | Gangschaltug, die | gearbox | la boîte de vitesses |
| 18 | cajetilla, la | Zigarettenschachtel, die | packet of cigaretes | le paquet de cigarettes |
| 5 | cajón, el | Schublade, die | drawer | le tiroir |
| 19 | calculado | kontrolliert | under control | préparé; organisé |
| 18 | calefacción, la | Heizung, die | heating | le chauffage |
| 7 | calentar | wärmen | to heat | chauffer |
| 13 | calidad, la | Qualität, die | quality | la qualité |
|  | calma, la | Ruhe, die | calm | le calme |
| 16 | calmante, el | Beruhigungsmittel, das | sedative | le calmant |
| 4 | calor, el | Hitze, die | heat | le chaleur |
| 6 | caluroso | heiß | hot | chaud |
| 13 | calzar | Schuhgröße haben Schuhe anziehen | to take size | chausser |
| 3 | calle, la | Straße, die | street | la rue |

| UNIDAD | ESPAÑOL | ALEMÁN | INGLÉS | FRANCÉS |
|---|---|---|---|---|
| 4 | cama, la | Bett, das | bed | le lit |
| 1 | camarero, el | Kellner, der | waiter | le serveur |
| 15 | cambiar(se) | (sich) umziehen | to (get) change(d) | se changer |
| 23 | camino, el | Weg, der | way | le chemin |
| 10 | camisa, la | Hemd, das | shirt | la chemise |
| 9 | campo, el | Land, das | countryside | la campagne |
| 2 | canadiense | kanadisch; Kanadier, der | Canadian | Canadien |
| 7 | canción, la | Lied, das | song | la chanson |
| 4 | cansado | müde | tired | fatigué |
| 13 | cantante, el/la | Sänger, der/-in, die | singer | le/la chanteur/euse |
| 7 | cantar | singen | to sing | chanter |
| 21 | cantidad, la | Summe, die | quantity | la quantité |
| 6 | caña de cerveza, la | ein Glas Bier, das | half pint of beer | un demi de bière |
| 4 | capital, la | Hauptstadt, die | capital | la capitale |
| 13 | capítulo, el | Kapitel, das | chapter | le chapitre |
| 9 | cara, la | Gesicht, das | face | le visage |
| 13 | carácter, el | Charakter, der | temperament; nature | le caractère |
| 8 | caramelo, el | Bonbon, das | sweet | le bonbon |
| 7 | cárcel, la | Gefägnis, das | prison | la prison |
| 22 | cariño, el | Zärtlichkeit, die | affection | l'affection |
| 20 | cariñoso | herzlich; liebevoll | loving; affectionate | affectueux |
| 13 | carne, la | Fleisch, das | meat | la viande |
| 2 | caro | teuer | expensive | cher |
| 19 | carrera, la | Studium, das | University degree | les études universitaires |
| 12 | carretera, la | Landstraße, die | road | la route |
|  | carro, el | Wagen, der | cart | le chariot |
| 7 | carta, la | Brief, der | letter | la lettre |
| 8 | cartero, el | Briefträger, der | postman | le facteur |
| 2 | casa, la | Haus, das | house | la maison |
| 5 | casado | verheiratet | married | marié |
| 16 | casar(se) | heiraten | to get married | (se) marier |
| 5 | caseta, la | Hundehütte, die | small house | la maisonnette |
| 9 | casi | fast | almost | presque |
| 17 | casino, el | Spielkasino, das | club; casino | le casino |
| 21 | castellano | castilisch; Kastilier, der | Castilian | le castillan |
| 17 | castillo, el | Burg, die | castle | le château |
| 3 | catedral, la | Dom, der | cathedral | la cathédrale |
| 20 | católico | katholisch; Katholik, der | catholic | catholique |
| 7 | cenar | zu Abend essen | to have dinner | dîner |
| 21 | central | zentral... | central | central |
| 4 | centro, el | Mitte, die | centre | le centre |
| 11 | cerámica, la | Keramik, die | ceramics; pottery | la céramique |
| 7 | cerca de | in der Nähe von; | near; next to | près de |

| UNIDAD | ESPAÑOL | ALEMÁN | INGLÉS | FRANCÉS |
|---|---|---|---|---|
| 4 | cerrado | geschlossen; zu | closed | fermé |
| 10 | cerradura, la | Schloß, das | lock | la serrure |
| 7 | cerrar | schließen | to close | fermer |
| 6 | cerveza, la | Bier, das | beer | la bière |
| 14 | césped, el | Rasen, der | lawn; grass | le gazon; la pelouse |
| 4 | cielo, el | Himmel, der | sky; heaven | le ciel |
| 4 | cien/ciento | hundert | hundred | cent |
| 19 | cierto | gewiß; sicher | sure; certain | certain |
| 7 | cigarrillo, el | Zigarette, die | cigarette | la cigarette |
| 7 | cigarro, el | Zigarre, die | cigar | le cigare |
| 1 | cinco | fünf | five | cinq |
| 2 | cincuenta | fünfzig | fifty | cinquante |
| 3 | cine, el | Kino, das | cinema | le cinema |
|  | ciprés, el | Zypresse, die | cypress | le cyprès |
| 19 | cita, la | Verabredung, die Termin, der | appointment; date | le rendez-vous |
| 9 | citar(se) con | (sich) verabreden mit | to have a date/ an appointment with | donner rendez-vous |
| 3 | ciudad, la | Stadt, die | city; town | la ville |
| 17 | civil | bürgerlich | civil | civil |
| 22 | claridad, la | Klarheit, die | clarity | la clarté |
| 6 | ¡claro! | klar! | sure!; of course! | bien sûr! |
| 3 | clase, la | Klassenzimmer, das | class | la classe |
| 9 | clásico | klassisch | classic | classique |
| 23 | cliente, el | Kunde, der | client | le client |
| 6 | clima, el | Klima, das | climate | le climat |
| 23 | clínica, la | Klinik, die | clinic | la clinique |
| 4 | cocina, la | Küche, die | kitchen | la cuisine |
| 2 | coche, el | Auto, das; Wagen, der | car | la voiture |
| 22 | coche-cama, el | Schlafwagen, der | sleeper | le wagon-lit |
| 14 | coger | nehmen | to take; to catch | prendre |
| 20 | cola, la | Schlange, die | queue | la queue |
| 17 | colección, la | Sammlung, die | collection | la collection |
| 9 | colegio, el | Schule, die | school | l'école |
| 7 | colgar | hängen | to hang | pendre |
| 5 | color, el | Farbe, die | colour | la couleur |
| 16 | collar, el | Halskette, die | necklace | le collier |
| 4 | comedor, el | Eßzimmer, das | dining room | la salle à manger |
| 7 | comenzar | anfangen; beginnen | to start | commencer |
| 7 | comer | essen | to eat | manger |
| 22 | comercial | Handels... | commercial | commercial |
| 2 | comida, la | Essen, das | food | la nourriture |
| 19 | comisaría, la | Polizeirevier, das | police station | le commissariat |
| 2 | ¿cómo? | wie? | how? | comment? |
| 18 | como | da | like; as | comme |

| UNIDAD | ESPAÑOL | ALEMÁN | INGLÉS | FRANCÉS |
|---|---|---|---|---|
| 22 | como mínimo | mindestens | at the very least | au minimun |
| 18 | comodidad, la | Bequemlichkeit, die | comfort | la commodité |
| 4 | cómodo | bequem | comfortable | confortable |
| 7 | compañero, el | Mitschüler, der | mate | le compagnon |
| 19 | compañía, la | Gesellschaft, die | company | la compagnie |
| 7 | complemento, el | Ergänzung, die | complement | le complément |
| 1 | completar | ergänzen | to complete | compléter |
|  | complicado | kompliziert | complicated | compliqué |
| 22 | componer | komponieren | to compose | composer |
| 5 | compra, la | Einkauf, der | purchase; buy | l'achat |
| 7 | comprar | kaufen | to buy; to purchase | acheter |
| 8 | comprender | verstehen | to understand | comprendre |
| 19 | comprobar | feststellen | to verify; to prove | vérifier |
| 23 | comunicado | verkehrsgünstig | served | desservi |
| 9 | comunicación, la | Verbindung, die | communication | la communication |
| 10 | comunicando | belegt; besetzt | engaged | occupé |
|  | comunicar con con | verbinden mit mit | to join; to connect with | communiquer avec |
| 8 | concierto, el | Konzert, das | concert | le concert |
| 20 | concurso, el | Wettbewerb, der | contest | le concours |
| 20 | condenar | verurteilen | to condemn; to find guilty | condamner |
| 22 | condición, la | Bedingung, die | condition | la condition |
| 10 | conducir | Auto fahren | to drive | conduire |
| 11 | conferencia, la | Konferenz, die; Vortrag, der | conference | la conférence |
| 7 | conferenciante, el | Redner, der | lecturer, speaker | le conférencier |
| 13 | confortable | komfortabel | comfortable | confortable |
| 6 | congreso, el | Kongreß, der | congress | le congrès |
| 17 | conmemorar | gedenken | to commemorate | commémorer |
| 8 | conmigo | mit mir | with me | avec moi |
| 10 | conocer | kennenlernen; kennen | to know | connaître |
| 19 | conseguir | erreichen; gelingen | to get; to achieve | obtenir |
| 9 | consentir | erlauben; zulassen | to consent to; to allow | consentir |
| 4 | conservado | erhalten | preserved | conservé |
| 4 | consola, la | Konsole, die | console | la console |
|  | constituir | bilden | to constitute; to be | constituer |
| 17 | construir | bauen | to build | construire; bâtir |
| 10 | contaminación, la | Luftverschmutzung; Polution, die | pollution | la pollution |
| 7 | contar | (er) zählen | to count | compter |
| 23 | contar con | rechnen mit | to count on | compter sur |
| 4 | contento | zufrieden | happy; content | content |
| 8 | contestación, la | Antwort, die | answer | la réponse |

| UNIDAD | ESPAÑOL | ALEMÁN | INGLÉS | FRANCÉS |
|---|---|---|---|---|
| 1 | contestar | antworten | to answer | répondre |
| 8 | contigo | mit dir | with me | avec toi |
| 6 | continental | kontinental | continental | continental |
| 23 | continuamente | ständig | continuously | continuellement |
| 19 | contra | gegen | against | contre |
| 17 | contribuir | beitragen | to contribute | contribuer |
| 14 | control, el | Kontrolle, die | control | le contrôle |
| 23 | conveniente | nützlich; ratsam | suitable; advisable | convenable |
|  | conversación, la | Gespräch, das; | conversation | la conversation |
| 17 | conversar | sich unterhalten | to converse; to talk; to chat | parler |
| 16 | convocar | einberufen | to convoke; to call together | convoquer; réunir |
| 11 | convocatoria, la | Veranstaltung, die | convocation | la convocation |
|  | corazón, el | Herz, das | heart | le coeur |
| 5 | corbata, la | Krawatte, die | tie | la cravate |
| 6 | corona, la | Krone, die | crown | la couronne |
| 9 | corregir | korrigieren; verbessern | to correct | corriger |
| 12 | correo, el | Post, die | post | la Poste |
| 8 | correr | rennen | run | courir |
| 23 | correspondencia, la | Briefwechsel, der Korrespondez; Post, die | correspondence | la correspondance |
| 18 | corrida, la | Stierkampf, der | bullfight | la corrida |
| 6 | cortado, el | Kaffee mit wenig Milch | coffee with a drop of milk | le café avec un peu du lait |
| 9 | cortar | schneiden | to cut | couper |
| 6 | corto | kurz | short | court |
| 19 | cosa, la | Sache, die | thing | la chose |
| 20 | cosecha, la | Ernte, die | crop; harvest | la récolte |
| 6 | costa, la | Küste, die | coast | la côte |
| 6 | costar | kosten | to cost | coûter |
| 18 | costilla, la | Rippe, die | rib | la côte |
| 20 | costumbre, la | Sitte, die | customs | les moeurs |
| 10 | crecer | wachsen | to grow | croître; grandir |
| 16 | crccr | glaubcn | to think; to bclicvc | croirc |
| 3 | crisis, la | Krise, die | crisis | la crise |
| 17 | cristal, el | Kristall, der | glass | le cristal |
| 20 | crítica, la | Kritik, die | criticism | la critique |
| 11 | crítico, el | Kritiker, der | critic | le critique |
| 6 | cronológico | chronologisch | chronological | chronologique |
| 22 | crucero, el | Kreuzfahrt, die | liner, cruise | la croisière |
| 7 | cruzar | überqueren | to cross | croiser |
| 10 | cuaderno, el | Heft, das | notebook | le cahier |
| 4 | cuadrado | quadratisch; viereckig | square | carré |
| 4 | cuadro, el | Bild, das | painting | le tableau |

| UNIDAD | ESPAÑOL | ALEMÁN | INGLÉS | FRANCÉS |
|---|---|---|---|---|
| 6 | ¿cuál? | welcher, e, es? | which? | quel? |
| 21 | cualquier | irgendein, e | any | n'importe qui |
| 6 | ¿cuándo? | wann? | when? | Quand? |
| 15 | cuando | als; wenn | when | quand; lorsque |
| 6 | ¿cuánto? | wieviel? | How much/many? | combien de? |
| 2 | cuarenta | vierzig | forty | quarante |
| 13 | cuarto | viert… | fourth | quatrième |
| 18 | cuarto de estar, el | Wohnzimmer, das | sitting room | la salle de séjour |
| 6 | cuarto, un | Viertel, ein | room | la chambre |
| 1 | cuatro | vier | four | quatre |
| 6 | cuatrocientos | vierhundert | four hundred | quatre cents |
| 2 | cubano | kubanisch; Kubaner, der | Cuban | cubain |
| 20 | cubierto, el | Besteck, das | set of cutlery | le couvert |
| 18 | cubrir(se) | (sich) bedecken | to be covered | se couvrir |
| 7 | cuenta, la | Rechnung, die | bill | le compte |
| 8 | cuento, el | Märchen, das | tale | le conte |
| 22 | cuidado, el | Achtung, die; Vorsicht, der | care | la prudence |
| 21 | culpable | schuldig | guilty | coupable |
| 11 | cultural | kulturell | cultural | culturel |
| 6 | cumpleaños, el | Geburtstag, der | birthday | l'anniversaire |
| 19 | cumplir años | alt werden | to reach the age of | être l'anniversaire de |
|  | cuna, la | Wiege, die | cradle | le berceau |
| 5 | cuñado | Schwager, der | brother-in-law | le beau-frère |
| 23 | curar(se) | heilen gesund werden | to be cured of; to recover from | se soigner |
| 13 | curso, el | Kurs, der; (Hoch) shuljahr, das | course; academic year | le cours; l'anné academique |

## CH

| UNIDAD | ESPAÑOL | ALEMÁN | INGLÉS | FRANCÉS |
|---|---|---|---|---|
| 21 | chalet, el | Landhaus, das; Villa, die | chalet | la villa |
| 5 | chaqueta, la | Jacke, die | jacket | la veste |
| 7 | charlar | schwatzen, plaudern | to talk; to chat | bavarder |
| 2 | checoslovaco | tschechoslowakisch; Tschechoslowake, der | Czechoslovak(ian) | Tchécoslovaque |
| 6 | chelín, el | Schilling, der | shilling | le shilling |
| 5 | chico, el | Junge; Kerl, der | boy | le garçon |
| 2 | chileno | chilenisch; Chilene, der | chilean | Chilien |
| 12 | chimenea, la | Kamin, der | chimney | la cheminée |
| 2 | chino | chinesisch; Chinese, der | Chinese | chinois |
| 13 | chiste, el | Witz, der | joke | la blague |
| 9 | chocolate, el | Schokolade, die | chocolate | le chocolat |

## D

| UNIDAD | ESPAÑOL | ALEMÁN | INGLÉS | FRANCÉS |
|---|---|---|---|---|
| 17 | dama, la | Dame, die | lady | la dame |
| 2 | danés | dänisch; Däne, der | Danish | danois |
| 7 | dar | geben | to give | donner |
| 15 | dar un paseo | einen Spaziergang machen | to go for a walk | faire une promenade |
| 14 | darse prisa | sich beeilen | to hurry; to rush | se hâter; se dépêcher |
| 2 | de | aus; von | from; of (several other prepositions) | de |
| 8 | de acuerdo | einverstanden | all right | d'accord |
| 22 | de antelación | im voraus; vorher | before; in advance | à l'avance |
| 4 | debajo de | unter | under; below | sous; en dessous de |
| 11 | deber | sollen | must | devoir |
| 15 | deberes, los | Hausaufgaben, die | homework | les devoirs |
| 5 | débil | schwach | weak | faible |
| 20 | de cabeza | kopfüber; sofort | headfirst; quickly, direct | la tête; la première |
| 6 | decena, la | Zehner, der | dozen | la dizaine |
| 18 | decidir(se) | sich entschließen | to make up one's mind | se décider |
| 13 | décimo | Zehnt, der, die, das | tenth | dixième |
| 9 | decir | sagen | to say; to tell | dire |
| 19 | declaración, la | Aussage, die | declaration | la déclaration |
| 14 | declarar | erklären, verzollen | to declare | déclarer |
| 21 | decorador, el | Dekorateur, der | decorator | le décorateur |
| 21 | decorar | dekorieren | to decorate | décorer |
| 16 | dedicarse | sich widmen, sich bestreben | to dedicate; to devote oneself to | se consacrer |
| 2 | ¿de dónde? | woher? | where from? | d'où? |

| UNIDAD | ESPAÑOL | ALEMÁN | INGLÉS | FRANCÉS |
|---|---|---|---|---|
| 17 | deducir | erschließen | to deduce | déduire |
| 8 | defender | verteidigen | to defend | défendre |
| 8 | dejar | leihen | to lend; to borrow | laisser |
| 20 | dejar de | aufhören mit | stop + gerund | cesser de; arrêter |
| 4 | delante de | vor | before; in front of | devant |
| 2 | delgado | schlank | thin | mince |
| 21 | delicioso | köstlich; | delicious | délicieux |
| 12 | demasiado | zuviel | too much | trop |
| 7 | demostrar | beweisen | to demonstrate; to prove | démontrer |
| 14 | dentista, el | Zahnarzt, der | dentist | le dentiste |
| 4 | dentro de | in | inside | dans |
| 19 | denunciar | eine Anzeige machen | to report; to give notice of | dénoncer |
| 13 | dependiente, el | Verkäufer, der | shop assistant | le vendeur; le commis |
| 14 | deporte, el | Sport, der | sport | le sport |
| 17 | deportista, el/la | Sportler, der/-in, die | sportsperson, athlete | une personne sportive |
| 11 | deportista | sportlich | sporting | sportif |
| 6 | deprisa | schnell | quickly; fast | vite |
| 5 | ¿de qué color es? | welche Farbe hat…? | What colour is it? | De quelle couleur est…? |
| 4 | derecha, la | die rechte Seite; rechts | right | la droite |
| 20 | de repente | plötzlich | suddenly | soudain; subitement |
| 6 | desagradable | unangenehm | disagreeable | désagréable |
| 18 | desayunar | frühstücken | to have breakfast | déjeuner |
| 14 | desayuno, el | Frühstück, das | breakfast | le petit déjeuner |
| 12 | descansar | ausruhen | to rest | reposer |
| 6 | descanso, el | Pause, die | rest, break | le repos |
| 23 | descender | (herab) (hinunter) steigen; sinken | to descend; to go down | descendre |
| 15 | descripción, la | Beschreibung, die | description | la description |
| 6 | desde | seit | since | depuis |
| 15 | ¡desde luego! | selbstverständlich | of course! | bien sûr! |
| 7 | desear | wünschen | to wish | souhaiter |
| 23 | deseo, el | Wunsch, der | wish | le désir |
| 9 | desnudar(se) | (sich) ausziehen | to undress | se déshabiller |
| 4 | desordenado | unordentlich | untidy; in a mess | désordonné |
| 17 | despacio | langsam | slow | lentement |
| 4 | despacho, el | Arbeitszimmer, das | office | le bureau |
| 9 | despedir(se) | sich verabschieden | to say goodbye | faire ses adieux à |
| 6 | despejado | heiter; wolkenlos | clear; cloudless | dégagé |
| 7 | despertador, el | Wecker, der | alarm clock | le réveil |
| 7 | despertar(se) | (auf)wecken; aufwachen | to wake up | se réveiller |
| 18 | despierto | wach | awake | réveillé |
| 16 | desprender(se) | hinabstürzen | to become detached; to fall off | se détacher |

| UNIDAD | ESPAÑOL | ALEMÁN | INGLÉS | FRANCÉS |
|---|---|---|---|---|
| 11 | después de | nach | after | après |
| 17 | destacar | hervorheben | to stand out | faire remarquer |
| 14 | destino, el | Schicksal, das | destination | la destination |
| 17 | destruir | zerstören | to destroy | détruire |
| 19 | de todas formas | auf jeden Fall | anyway | de toute façon |
| 4 | detrás de | hinter | behind | derrière |
| 12 | de vez en cuando | ab und zu; manchmal | now and again | de temps en temps |
| 8 | devolver | zurückgeben | to give back | rendre |
| 6 | día, el | Tag, der | day | le jour |
| 17 | diariamente | täglich | daily | journellement |
| 5 | diccionario, el | Wörterbuch, das | dictionary | le dictionnaire |
| 6 | diciembre | Dezember, der | December | décembre |
| 8 | dictar | diktieren | to dictate | dicter |
| 1 | diecinueve | neunzehn | nineteen | dix-neuf |
| 1 | dieciocho | achtzehn | eighteen | dix-huit |
| 1 | dieciséis | sechzehn | sixteen | seize |
| 1 | diecisiete | siebzehn | seventeen | dix-sept |
| 9 | diente, el | Zahn, der | tooth | la dent |
| 12 | dieta, la | Diät, die | diet | le régime |
| 1 | diez | zehn | ten | dix |
| 10 | difícil | schwer | difficult | difficile |
| 21 | dificultad, la | Schwierigkeit, die | difficulty | la difficulté |
| 12 | digestión, la | Verdauung, die | digestion | la digestion |
| 5 | dinero, el | Geld, das | money | l'argent |
| 8 | dirección, la | Adresse, die | address | la direction |
| 3 | director, el | Direktor, der | director | le directeur |
| 15 | director de cine, el | Regisseur, der | cinema director | le metteur en scène |
| 14 | dirigir(se) | sich begeben | to go to; to head to | gagner |
| 8 | disco, el | Schallplatte, die | record | le disque |
| 23 | discriminado | diskriminiert | discriminated | discriminé |
| 22 | discurso, el | Rede, die | discourse | le discours |
| 22 | discutir | diskutieren | to discuss; to debate | discuter |
| 16 | dislocado | verrenkt | dislocated | disloqué; démis |
| 21 | disponer de | verfügen über | to have at one's disposal | disposer de |
| 23 | dispuesto | bereit | disposed | disposé |
| 17 | distraer | unterhalten | to distract | distraire |
| 9 | divertir(se) | (sich) amüsieren; unterhalten | to enjoy (oneself) | (s)'amuser |
| 5 | divorciado | geschieden | divorced | divorcé |
| 1 | doce | zwölf | twelve | douze |
| 12 | doctor, el | Arzt; Doktor, der | doctor | le docteur |
| 6 | dólar, el | Dollar, der | dollar | le dollar |
| 8 | doler | schmerzen; weh tun | to hurt; to ache | avoir mal; faire mal |

| UNIDAD | ESPAÑOL | ALEMÁN | INGLÉS | FRANCÉS |
|---|---|---|---|---|
| 12 | dolor de cabeza, el | Kopfschmerz, der | headache | le mal de tête |
| 6 | domingo, el | Sonntag, der | Sunday | Dimanche |
| 3 | dominó, el | Domino, das | domino | le domino |
| 2 | ¿dónde? | wo? | where? | où? |
| 9 | dormir(se) | (ein) schlafen | (to fall) sleep | (s)'endormir |
| 4 | dormitorio, el | Schlafzimmer, das | bedroom | la chambre |
| 1 | dos | zwei | two | deux |
| 6 | doscientos | zweihundert | two hundred | deux cents |
| 6 | dos mil | zweitausend | two thousand | deux mille |
| 15 | drogadicto, el | Drogensüchtige, der | drug addict | attaché à la drogue |
| 9 | duchar(se) | (sich) duschen | to have a shower | prende une douche |
| 19 | duda, la | Zweifel, der | doubt | le doute |
| 21 | dueño, el | Besitzer, der | owner | le maître |
| 19 | dulce | süß | sweet | doux |
| 13 | duodécimo | Zwölfte… / Zwölfter, das | twelfth | douzième |
|  | dúo, el | Duo; Duett, das | duet; duo | le duo |
| 7 | durante | während | during; for | pendant |
| 6 | durar | dauern | to last | durer |

# E

| UNIDAD | ESPAÑOL | ALEMÁN | INGLÉS | FRANCÉS |
|---|---|---|---|---|
| 10 | económico | ökonomisch; wirtschaftlich | economical | économique |
| 2 | ecuatoriano | ecuadorianisch; Ecuadorianer, der | Ecuadorean | Équatorien |
| 12 | echarse la siesta | Siesta halten | to have a sleep | faire la sieste |
| 6 | edad, la | Alter, das | age | l' âge |
| 3 | edificio, el | Gebäude, das | building | l'édifice, le bâtiment |
| 23 | eficazmente | tüchtig | efficaciously | efficacement |
| 2 | egipcio | ägyptisch; Ägypter, der | Egiptian | Égyptien |
| 8 | ejercicio, el | Übung, die | exercise | l'exercice |
| 1 | él | er | he | il |
| 5 | elegante | elegant | elegant | élégant |
| 13 | elegir | auswählen | to choose | choisir |
| 14 | embarque, el | Abfertigung, die | board | l' embarquement |
| 7 | empezar | anfangen; beginnen | to start | commencer |
| 23 | empleado, el | Angestellte, der | employee | l'employé |
| 1 | empleo, el | Arbeitsstelle, die | employ | l'emploi |
| 7 | empresa, la | Firma, die | firm | l'entreprise |
| 18 | empujón, el | Stoß, der | push | la poussée |
| 4 | en | in | in/on/at (and other prep.) | en/à/dans |
| 18 | enamorar(se) de | sich verlieben in | to fall in love with | tomber amoureux |
| 1 | encantado | es freut mich; sehr angenehm | nice to meet you | enchanté |
| 18 | encargar | bestellen | to ask for; to order | demander; commander |
| 8 | encender | anmachen | to turn on | allumer |

| UNIDAD | ESPAÑOL | ALEMÁN | INGLÉS | FRANCÉS |
|---|---|---|---|---|
| 7 | encerrar | einschließen; | to lock | enfermer |
| 21 | encima | darauf; oben | above; over | dessus; sur |
| 11 | encontrar | finden | to find | trouver |
| 16 | en el acto | plötzlich; sofort | immediately | sur le coup |
| 18 | energía, la | Energie, die | energy | l'énergie |
| 4 | enero | Januar, der | January | Janvier |
| 4 | enfadado | ärgerlich; böse | angry | fâché |
| 15 | enfermedad, la | Krankheit, die | illness | la maladie |
| 1 | enfermera, la | Krankenschwester, die | nurse | l'infirmière |
| 7 | enfrente de | gegenüber | opposite to | en face de |
| 20 | engordar | dicker werden; zunehmen | to put on weight | grossir |
| 11 | en ningún lado | nirgendswo | nowhere | nulle part |
| 6 | en punto | pünktlich | punctually | juste/pile |
| 8 | ensalada, la | Salat, der | salad | la salade |
| 6 | enseguida | gleich; sofort | at once; straight away | tout de suite |
| 7 | enseñanza, la | Ausbildung, die; Unterrichtswesen, das | education; teaching | l'enseignement |
| 8 | enseñar | zeigen | to show | enseigner |
| 9 | ensuciar | beschmutzen; | to soil | salir |
| 8 | entender | verstehen | to understand | comprendre |
| 16 | enterar(se) | erfahren | to get to know; to find out | s' informer |
| 6 | entonces | dann | then | alors |
| 6 | entrada, la | Eintrittskarte, die | ticket | l' entrée |
| 19 | entrar | eintreten | to enter; to go in | entrer |
| 12 | entre | zwischen | between; among | entre |
| 14 | entregar | abgeben | to hand over | remettre |
| 17 | entrenar(se) | trainieren | to train; to coach | s'entraîner |
| 22 | entretener(se) | sich aufhalten lassen; sich unterhalten | to hold up | se mettre en retard |
| 14 | entretiempo | Übergangs… | period between seasons | la demi-saison |
| 22 | entusiasmo, el | Begeisterung, die | enthusiasm | l' enthousiasme |
| 8 | envolver | einpacken | to wrap up | envelopper |
| 14 | equipaje, el | Gepäck, das | luggage | les bagages |
| 13 | equipo, el | Mannschaft, die | team | l'équipe |
| 21 | equivocarse | sich irren | to make a mistake | se tromper |
| 9 | escalar | klettern | to climb | escalader |
| 4 | escalera, la | Treppe, die | staircase | l'escalier |
| 7 | escaparate, el | Schaufenster, das | shop window | la vitrine |
| 8 | esconder(se) | (sich) verstecken | to hide oneself from | se cacher |
| 9 | escribir | schreiben | to write | écrire |
| 7 | escuchar | hören | to listen to | écouter |
| 14 | escuela, la | Schule, die | school | l'école |
| 3 | ese | der da | that | ce-là |
| 23 | esencial | Wesentlich | essential | essentiel |
| 1 | español | spanisch; Spanier, der | Spanish | espagnol |

| UNIDAD | ESPAÑOL | ALEMÁN | INGLÉS | FRANCÉS |
|---|---|---|---|---|
| 8 | especialidad, la | Spezialität, die | speciality | la spécialité |
| 11 | espectáculo, el | Aufführung, die; Show, die | show | le spectacle |
| 20 | espectador, el | Zuschauer, der | spectator | le spectateur |
| 10 | espejo, el | Spiegel, der | mirror | le miroir |
| 7 | esperar | warten | to wait | attendre |
| 17 | espeso | dicht | thick | épais |
| 15 | esquiar | skifahren | to ski | skier |
| 7 | esquina, la | Ecke, die | corner | le coin |
| 3 | estación, la | Bahnhof, der | station | la gare |
| 6 | estación del año, la | Jahreszeit, die | season | la saison |
| 12 | estadio, el | Stadium, das | stadium | le stade |
| 4 | estado, el | Zustand, der | state | l'état |
| 2 | estado, el | Staat, der | State | l'État |
| 14 | estancia, la | Aufenthalt, der | stay | le séjour |
| 16 | estanque, el | Teich, der | pond | l' étang |
|  | estantería, la | Regal, das | shelf | le rayonnage; les étagères |
| 4 | estar | sein | to be | être |
| 4 | estar de pie | stehen | to stand up | être debout |
| 4 | estar en forma | in Form sein | to be fit | être en pleine forme |
| 3 | este | dieser, der hier | this | ce-ci |
| 16 | este, el | Osten, der | east | l'est |
| 17 | estilo, el | Stil, der | style | le style |
| 8 | estómago, el | Bauch, der | stomach | l'estomac |
| 10 | estropeado | beschädigt | damaged; spoiled | abîmé; gâché |
| 17 | estropear(se) | kaputt gehen | to get damaged | s'abîmer |
| 1 | estudiante, el/la | Student, der/-in, die | student | l'étudiant |
| 7 | estudiar | lernen, studieren | to study | étudier |
| 10 | estudio, el | Studie; Untersuchung, die | research | l'étude |
| 7 | estudios, los | Studium, das | schooling | les études |
| 13 | estupendo | ausgezeichnet; | splendid | excellent; extraordinaire |
| 22 | exactamente | genau | exactly | exactement |
| 18 | exagerar | übertreiben | to exaggerate | exagérer |
| 6 | examen, el | Examen, das; Prüfung, die | exam | l'examen |
| 27 | examinar | prüfen | to examine | examiner |
| 16 | examinarse de | eine Prüfung in ... ablegen | to take an examination in | passer un examen de |
| 14 | exceso, el | Übergewicht, das | excess | l'excès |
| 17 | excluir | ausschließen | to exclude | exclure |
| 8 | excursión, la | Ausflug, der | excursion | l'excursion |
| 23 | exigir | fordern; verlangen | to demand; to call for | exiger |
| 7 | éxito, el | Erfolg, der | success | le succès |

| UNIDAD | ESPAÑOL | ALEMÁN | INGLÉS | FRANCÉS |
|---|---|---|---|---|
| 23 | experiencia, la | Erfahrung, die | experience | l'expérience |
| 7 | explicar | erklären | to explain | expliquer |
| 19 | explosión, la | Explosion, die | explosion | l'explosion |
| 7 | exportar | exportieren | to export | exporter |
| 11 | exposición, la | Ausstellung, die | exhibition | l'exposition |
| 3 | éxtasis, el | Ekstase, die | extasy | l'extase |
| 5 | extranjero | ausländisch | foreign | étranger |

# F

| UNIDAD | ESPAÑOL | ALEMÁN | INGLÉS | FRANCÉS |
|---|---|---|---|---|
| 3 | fábrica, la | Fabrik, die | factory | l'usine |
| 13 | fácil | leicht | easy | facile |
| 23 | factura, la | Rechnung, die | invoice; bill | la facture |
| 14 | facturar | abfertigen | to check in | enregistrer |
| 23 | facultad, la | Fakultät, die | Faculty; | la Faculté |
| 5 | falda, la | Rock, der | skirt | la jupe |
| 19 | falso | falsch | false | faux |
| 9 | falta, la | Fehler, der | mistake | la faute |
| 5 | familia, la | Familie, die | family | la famille |
| 17 | famoso | berühmt | famous | fameux / célèbre |
| 10 | favor, el | Gefallen, der | favour | la faveur |
| 6 | febrero | Februar, der | February | Février |
| 17 | fecha, la | Datum, das | date | la date |
| 14 | feliz | angenehm | happy | heureux |
| 22 | felizmente | glücklicherweise | happily | heureusement |
| 14 | fiebre, la | Fieber, das | fever | la fièvre |
| 4 | fiesta, la | Feiertag, der; Party, die | party | la fête |
| 6 | Fiesta Nacional, la | Nationalfeiertag, der | bank holiday; public holiday | la fête nationale |
| 13 | fila, la | Reihe, die | row | le rang |
| 23 | filial, la | Tochterfirma, die | subsidiary company | la filiale |
| 4 | final, el | Ende, das | end | la fin |
| 9 | fin de semana, el | Wochenende, das | weekend | le weekend |
| 7 | firmar | unterschreiben | to sign | signer |
| 4 | físico | physisch | physical | physique |
| 13 | flamenco, el | Flamenco, der | flamenco singing | le chant flamenco |

| UNIDAD | ESPAÑOL | ALEMÁN | INGLÉS | FRANCÉS |
|---|---|---|---|---|
| 5 | flor, la | Blume, die | flower | la fleur |
| 14 | florecer | blühen | to flower | fleurir |
| 13 | folklore, el | Folklore, die | folklore | le folklore |
| 22 | folleto, el | Broschüre, die; | brochure; leaflet | la brochure |
| 21 | fondo, el | Ende, das | back; far end | le fond |
| 19 | forma, la | Form, die | form; shape | la forme |
| 16 | formar parte | gehören | to be a part of | faire partie de |
| 3 | fotografía, la | Fotografie, die | photography | la photographie |
| 2 | francés | französisch; Franzose, der | French | Français |
| 6 | franco, el | Franken, der | franc | le franc |
| 7 | fregar | spülen | to wash up | laver |
| 2 | frente a | gegenüber | opposite to; facing | en face de |
| 6 | fresa, la | Erdbeere, die | strawberry | la fraise |
| 17 | fresco | frisch | fresh | frais |
| 15 | frigorífico, el | Kühlschrank, der | fridge | le réfrigérateur |
| 6 | frío, el | Kälte, die | cold | froid |
| 8 | fruta del tiempo, la | frisches Obst | seasonal fruit | fruits de saison |
| 16 | frutero, el | Obstschale, die | fruit bowl | la coupe à fruits |
| 4 | fuego, el | Feuer, das | fire | le feu |
| 17 | fuente, la | Brunnen, der | fountain; spring | la fontaine |
| 4 | fuera de | außerhalb | out of | hors de |
| 5 | fuerte | kräftig; stark | strong | fort |
| 7 | fumar | rauchen | to smoke | fumer |
| 15 | funcionar | funktionieren | to function | fonctionner |
| 9 | fútbol, el | Fußballspiel, das | football | le football |
| 14 | futbolista, el | Fußballspieler, der | football player | le joueur de football |

## G

| UNIDAD | ESPAÑOL | ALEMÁN | INGLÉS | FRANCÉS |
|---|---|---|---|---|
| 5 | gabardina, la | Regenmantel, der | overcoat, mac | la gabardine |
| 5 | gafas, las | Brille, die | glasses | des lunettes |
| 6 | galleta, la | Keks, der | biscuit | le biscuit |
|  | gallo, el | Hahn, der | cock | le coq |
| 18 | ganar | gewinnnen | to win | gagner |
| 13 | ganas, las | Lust, die | desire, wish | l'envie |
| 4 | garaje, el | Garage, die | garage | le garage |
| 12 | garganta, la | Hals, der | throat | la gorge |
| 10 | gasolina, la | Benzin, das | petrol | l'essence |
| 13 | gastar | ausgeben | to spend | dépenser |
| 4 | gato, el | Katze, die | cat | le chat |
| 5 | gente, la | Leute, die | people | le monde |
| 10 | Geografía, la | Geografie, die | geography | la géographie |
| 17 | gimnasia, la | Gymnastik, die | gymnastics | la gymnastique |
| 7 | gobernar | regieren | to govern | gouverner |
| 7 | golondrina, la | Schwalbe, die | swallow | l' hirondelle |
| 2 | gordo | dick | fat | gros |
|  | gota, la | Tropfen, der | drop | la goutte |
| 3 | gótico | gotisch | gothic | gothique |
| 4 | gracias | danke | thank you | merci |
| 7 | gramática, la | Grammatik, die | grammar | la grammaire |
| 20 | gran/grande | groß | big; large | grand |
| 17 | granja, la | Bauernhof, der | farm | la ferme |
| 12 | grasa, la | Fett, das | fat | la graisse |
| 12 | grave | ernst | serious | grave |
| 2 | griego | griechisch; Grieche, der | Greek | Grec |
| 5 | gris | grau | grey | gris |

| UNIDAD | ESPAÑOL | ALEMÁN | INGLÉS | FRANCÉS |
|---|---|---|---|---|
| 23 | gritar | schreien | to cry; to scream | crier |
| 17 | grúa, la | Kran, der | tow-truck | la grue |
| 20 | grupo, el | Gruppe, die | group | le groupe |
| 5 | guante, el | Handschuh, der | glove | le gant |
| 9 | guapo | hübsch | good-looking | beau |
| 15 | guerra, la | Krieg, der | war | la guerre |
| 20 | guía, el/la | Reiseführer, der/-in, die | guide | le guide |
| 11 | guiñol, el | Puppentheater, das | puppet theatre | le guignol |
| 2 | güisqui | Whisky, der | whisky | le whisky |
| 10 | guitarra, la | Guitarre, die | guitar | la guitare |
| 9 | gustar | gern haben; gefallen | like | aimer; plaire |
|  | gutural | guttural; Kehl… | guttural | guttural |

# H

| UNIDAD | ESPAÑOL | ALEMÁN | INGLÉS | FRANCÉS |
|---|---|---|---|---|
| 5 | hay | es gibt | there is/are | il y a |
| 3 | habitación, la | Zimmer, das | room | la chambre |
| 4 | habitante, el | Einwohner, der | inhabitant | l' habitant |
| 7 | hablar | sprechen | to speak | parler |
| 4 | hacer | machen | to do; to make | faire |
| 6 | hacer buen/mal tiempo | gutes/schlechtes Wetter sein | to be good/ bad weather | faire beau/ mauvais temps |
| 6 | hacer calor | warm/heiß sein | to be hot | faire chaud |
| 21 | hacer caso | auf jmdn hören | to pay attention to; to take seriously | faire cas de |
| 20 | hacer cola | Schlange stehen | to queue | faire la queue |
| 6 | hacer frío | kalt sein | to be cold | faire froid |
| 17 | hacer noche | übernachten | to spend the night | faire nuit |
| 6 | hacer sol | die Sonne scheint | to be sunny | le soleil luit |
| 6 | hacer viento | windig sein | to be windy | faire du vent |
| 12 | hacia | nach | to; towards | vers |
| 3 | hacha, el | Axt, die | axe | la hache |
| 6 | hambre, el | Hunger, der | hunger | la faim |
|  | harina, la | Mehl, das | flour | la farine |
| 6 | hasta | bis | until; as far as | jusque |
| 20 | hasta el momento | bis jetzt | so far | jusqu`au moment |
| 22 | hasta luego | bis dann | see you later | à bientôt |
| 22 | hasta pronto | bis bald | see you soon | à tout à l'heure |
| 12 | helado, el | Eis, das | ice-cream | la glace |
|  | heno, el | Heu, das | hay | le foin |
| 19 | heredar | erben | to inherit | hériter |

| UNIDAD | ESPAÑOL | ALEMÁN | INGLÉS | FRANCÉS |
|---|---|---|---|---|
| 19 | herido, el | Verletzte, der | injured person | une persone blessée |
| 19 | herir | verletzen | to injure | blesser |
| 4 | hermano, el | Bruder, der | brother | le frère |
| 23 | hervir | kochen | to boil | bouillir |
| 2 | hijo, el | Sohn, der | son | le fils |
| 2 | hindú | Hindu, der | Hindu | hindou |
| 10 | historia, la | Geschichte, die | history | la histoire |
| 1 | ¡hola! | Hallo! | hello! | bonjour! |
| 2 | Holanda | Holland | Holland | Hollande |
| 2 | holandés | holländisch; Holländer, der | Dutch | Hollandais |
| 18 | hombre, el | Mann, der | man | l'homme |
| 17 | honor, el | Ehre, die | honour | l'honneur |
| 4 | hora, la | Stunde, die | time | l'heure |
| 21 | horno, el | Ofen, der | oven | le four |
| 20 | horrible | schrecklich | horrible | horrible |
| 20 | horror, el | Schrecken, der | horror; dread | l'horreur |
| 4 | hospital, el | Hospital, das | hospital | l'hôpital |
| 17 | hostal, el | Gasthaus, das | boarding house | l'hôtellerie |
| 2 | hotel, el | Hotel, das | hotel | l'hôtel |
| 4 | hoy | heute | today | aujourd'hui |
| 22 | huelga, la | Streik, der | strike | la grève |
| 10 | huir | fliehen | to run away | fuir |
| 6 | húmedo | feucht | wet; humid | humide |
| 11 | humo, el | Rauch, der | smoke | la fumée |
| 9 | humor, el | Humor, der | mood; humour | l'humeur |
| 17 | humor de perros, un | schlechte Laune | bad mood | l' humeur de chien |
| 2 | húngaro | ungarisch; Ungar, der | Hungarian | Hongrois |

# I

| UNIDAD | ESPAÑOL | ALEMÁN | INGLÉS | FRANCÉS |
|---|---|---|---|---|
| 7 | idioma, el | Sprache, die | language | la langue |
| 3 | iglesia, la | Kirche, die | church | l'église |
| 7 | igualmente | gleichfalls | equally | également |
| 18 | imaginar(se) | sich vorstellen | to imagine | imaginer |
| 17 | impedir | verhindern | to impede; to prevent s. o. from doing something | empêcher |
| 15 | importante | wichtig | important | important |
| 22 | importe, el | Betrag, der | value; cost | le prix; la valeur |
| 23 | imposible | unmöglich | impossible | impossible |
| 22 | impresión, la | Eindruck, der | impression | l'impression |
| 18 | impreso, el | Formular, das | form | l'imprimé |
| 17 | impuesto, el | Steuer, die | tax | l'impôt |
| 18 | inaugurar | eröffnen | to inaugurate | inaugurer |
| 23 | incierto | ungewiß; unsicher | uncertain | incertain |
| 17 | incluir | einschließen | to include | inclure |
| 18 | incomodidad, la | Umbequemlichkeit, die | discomfort | l'incommodité |
| 4 | incómodo | unbequem | uncomfortable | incommode |
| 17 | inconveniente, no tener | nights dagegen haben | to have no objection | ne pas avoir d'inconvénient à |
| 21 | individual | einzel, persönlich | individual | individuel |
| 15 | industrial | industriell | industrial | industriel |
| 3 | industria, la | Industrie, die | industry | l'industrie |
| 15 | infancia, la | Kindheit, die | childhood | l'enfance |
| 22 | información, la | Information, die | information | l'information |
| 16 | informar(se) | sich informieren | to inform o. s.; to find out | s'informer |
| 17 | ingeniería, la | Ingenieurbau, der | engineering | le génie |
| 1 | ingeniero, el | Ingenieur, der | engineer | l'ingénieur |

| UNIDAD | ESPAÑOL | ALEMÁN | INGLÉS | FRANCÉS |
|---|---|---|---|---|
| 2 | inglés | englisch; Engländer, der | English | Anglais |
| 16 | ingresar | einliefern | to be admitted into (hospital) | être admis |
| 16 | inmediatamente | sofort | immediately | immédiatement |
| 16 | inquieto | unruhig | restless | inquiet |
| 21 | instalar(se) | installieren | to install; to set up | installer |
| 23 | insultar | beschimpfen | to insult | insulter |
| 13 | inteligente | intelligent; klug | intelligent | intelligent |
| 17 | intenso | dicht | intense | intense |
| 16 | intentar | versuchen | to try | essayer |
| 3 | interesante | interessant | interesting | intéressant |
| 18 | interesarse por | sich interessieren für | to become interested in | s'intéresser |
| 17 | interior, el | Innere, das | interior, inside | l'intérieur |
| 10 | introducir | einführen | to introduce | introduire |
| 19 | investigación, la | Untersuchung, die | investigation; inquiry | l'investigation |
| 14 | invierno, el | Winter, der | winter | l'hiver |
| 9 | invitado, el | Gast, der | guest | l'hôte |
| 7 | invitar | einladen | to invite | inviter |
| 6 | ir | gehen; fahren | to go | aller |
| 9 | ir a los toros | zur Stierkampfarena gehen | to go to the bullfight | aller aux courses des taureaux |
| 22 | ir de compras | einkaufen gehen | to go shopping | faire des courses |
| 2 | iraní | iranisch; Iraner, der | Iranian | Iranien |
| 2 | iraquí | irakisch; Irakaner, der | Iraqui | Irakien |
| 2 | israelita | israelitisch; Israelit, der | Israeli | Israélien |
| 2 | italiano | italienisch; Italiener, der | Italian | Italien |
| 17 | itinerario, el | (Reise) Route, die | itinerary; route | l'itinéraire |
| 4 | izquierda, la | linke Seite, die; links | left | la gauche |

## J

| UNIDAD | ESPAÑOL | ALEMÁN | INGLÉS | FRANCÉS |
|---|---|---|---|---|
| 18 | jamás | niemals | never | jamais |
| 6 | jamón, el | Schinken, der | ham | le jambon |
| 2 | japonés | japanisch; Japaner, der | Japonese | Japonais |
| 13 | jarabe, el | Sirup, der | syrup | le sirop |
| 4 | jardín, el | Garten, der | garden | le jardin |
| 11 | jarrón, el | Vase, die | vase | la potiche; le vase |
| 10 | jefe, el | Chef, der | chief; head; boss | le chef |
| 5 | jersey, el | Pullover, der | sweater; jumper pullover | le pull-over |
| 4 | joven | jung | young | jeune |
| 16 | joya, la | Juwel, das | jewel | le bijou |
| 11 | juego, el | Spiel, der | game | le jeu |
| 6 | jueves, el | Donnerstag, der | Thursday | Jeudi |
| 16 | juez, el | Richter, der | judge | le juge |
| 23 | jugador, el | Spieler, der | player | le joueur |
| 10 | jugar | spielen | to play | jouer |
| 13 | jugoso | saftig | juicy succulent | juteux; savoureux |
| 6 | julio | Juli, der | July | Juillet |
| 6 | junio | Juni, der | June | Juin |
| 12 | junto a | bei; neben | next to; by | près de; auprès de |
| 11 | juntos | zusammen | together | ensemble |

## K

| UNIDAD | ESPAÑOL | ALEMÁN | INGLÉS | FRANCÉS |
|---|---|---|---|---|
| 6 | kilo, el | Kilo, das | kilo | le kilo |
| 21 | kilómetro | Kilometer, der | kilometre | le kilomètre |

## L

| UNIDAD | ESPAÑOL | ALEMÁN | INGLÉS | FRANCÉS |
|---|---|---|---|---|
|  | labio, el | Lippe, die | lip | la lèvre |
| 8 | ladrón, el | Dieb, der | thief | le voleur |
| 22 | lágrima, la | Träne, die | tear | la larme |
| 4 | lámpara, la | Lampe, die | lamp | la lampe |
| 16 | lana, la | Wolle, die | wool | la laine |
| 4 | lápiz, el | Bleistift, der | pencil | le crayon |
| 9 | largo | lang | long | long |
| 9 | lavar(se) | (sich) waschen | to wash; to have a wash | se laver |
| 6 | leche, la | Milch, die | milk | le lait |
| 8 | leer | lesen | to read | lire |
| 7 | lejos de | weit von | far away from | loin de |
| 3 | lento | langsam | slow | lent |
| 4 | leña, la | (Brenn) holz, das | firewood | le bois de chauffage/à brûler |
| 17 | lesión, la | Verletzung, die | lesion | la lésion/le blessure |
| 9 | levantar(se) | aufstehen | to get up | se lever |
| 21 | libertad, la | Freiheit, die | freedom | la liberté |
| 6 | libra, la | Pfund, das | pound | la livre |
| 4 | libre | frei | free | libre |
| 3 | libro, el | Buch, das | book | le livre |
| 10 | licenciatura, la | akademische Grad, die | university degree | la maîtrise |
| 13 | limón, el | Zitrone, die | lemon | le citron |
| 10 | limpiar | putzen; sauber machen | to clean | nettoyer |
| 4 | limpio | sauber | clean | propre |
| 14 | línea, la | Linie, die | line | la ligne |
| 22 | listo | bereit; fertig | ready | prêt |
| 6 | litro, el | Liter, das | litre | le litre |

| UNIDAD | ESPAÑOL | ALEMÁN | INGLÉS | FRANCÉS |
|---|---|---|---|---|
| 18 | localidad, la | Eintrittskarte, die | locality; town | la localité |
| 19 | lógico | logisch | logical | logique |
| 19 | lograr | erreichen; gelingen | to get; to achieve; to obtain | obtenir; remporter |
| 20 | lo que | was | what | ce qui; ce que |
| 20 | lotería, la | Lotterie, die | lottery | la loterie |
| 21 | luchar | kämpfen | to fight | lutter |
| 3 | lunes, el | Montag, der | Monday | Lundi |
| 12 | luz, la | Licht, das | light | la lumière |

## LL

| UNIDAD | ESPAÑOL | ALEMÁN | INGLÉS | FRANCÉS |
|---|---|---|---|---|
| 9 | llamar | klingeln; klopfen | to knock; to ring | sonner; frapper à la porte |
| 10 | llave, la | Schlüssel, der | key | la clé |
| 16 | llegar | ankommen | to come; to arrive | arriver |
| 18 | lleno | voll | full | plein; rempli |
| 7 | llevar | mitnehmen | to carry; to bring; to take | porter; emporter; emmener |
| 6 | llover | regnen | to rain | pleuvoir |
|  | lluvia, la | Regen, der | rain | la pluie |

## M

| UNIDAD | ESPAÑOL | ALEMÁN | INGLÉS | FRANCÉS |
|---|---|---|---|---|
| 16 | madera, la | Holz, das | wood | le bois |
| 5 | madre, la | Mutter, die | mother | la mère |
|  | madrugada, la | Tagesanbruch, der; früher Morgen | early morning | l'aube; le petit jour |
| 6 | maduro | reif | ripe | mûr |
| 16 | maestro, el | Lehrer, der | teacher | le maître d'école |
| 6 | mal | schlecht | bad | mauvais |
| 17 | mala suerte, la | Pech, das | bad luck | la malchance |
| 10 | maleta, la | Koffer, der | suitcase | la valise |
| 22 | maletín, el | Handkoffer, der | briefcase | la serviette |
| 13 | malo | schlecht | bad | mauvais |
| 11 | mandar | schicken | to order; to command | ordonner; commander |
| 12 | manga, la | Ärmel, der | sleeve | la manche |
| 9 | mano, la | Hand, die | hand | la main |
| 8 | manzana, la | Apfel, der | apple | la pomme |
| 6 | mañana, la | Morgen, der | morning | le matin |
| 10 | máquina, la | Maschine, die | machine | la machine |
| 9 | mar, el/la | Meer, das; See, die | sea | la mer |
| 17 | maravilloso | wunderbar | wonderful | merveilleux |
| 13 | marcar | kosten | to cost | coûter |
| 6 | marco, el | Mark, die | mark | le mark |
| 12 | marchar(se) | weggehen; wegfahren | to go (away); to leave | s'en aller; partir |
| 5 | marido, el | Ehemann, der | husband | le mari |
| 5 | marrón | braun | brown | marron |
| 2 | marroquí | marokkanisch; Marokkaner, der | Moroccan | Marocain |

| UNIDAD | ESPAÑOL | ALEMÁN | INGLÉS | FRANCÉS |
|---|---|---|---|---|
| 4 | martes, el | Dienstag, der | Tuesday | Mardi |
| 6 | marzo | März, der | March | Mars |
| 20 | más | mehr | more | plus |
| 16 | matemáticas, las | Mathematik, die | mathematics | les mathématiques |
| 10 | material, el | Material, das | material | le matériel |
| 17 | matrícula, la | Immatrikulation, die | register | l'inscription |
| 17 | matriculado | immatrikuliert | registered | inscrit |
| 6 | mayo | Mai, der | May | Mai |
| 5 | mayor | der, die, das älteste | the eldest | l'aîne |
| 5 | mecánico, el | Mechaniker, der | mechanic | le mécanicien |
| 16 | media, la | Strumpf, der | stockings | les bas |
| 13 | medicina, la | Arznei, die | medicine | la médicine |
| 1 | médico, el | Arzt, der | Doctor | le médecin |
| 16 | medida, la | Maßnahme, die | measure | la mesure |
| 6 | medio, el | Mittel, das | means; way | le moyen |
| 18 | medio de transporte, el | Verkehrsmittel, das | means of transport | les moyens de transport |
| 6 | mediodía, el | Mittag, der | midday | le midi |
| 6 | medio kilo | halbes Kilo | half kilo | demi kilo |
| 9 | medir | messen | to measure | mesurer |
| 2 | mejicano | mexikanisch; Mexikaner, der | Mexican | Mexicain |
| 4 | mejor | besser | better | meilleur; mieux |
| 16 | mejorar(se) | sich bessern, gute Besserung! | to get better; to improve | s'améliorer |
| 10 | memoria de licenciatura, la | Diplomarbeit, die | dissertation; thesis | le mémoire de la licence |
| 5 | menor, el | der, die, das jüngste | the youngest | le plus petit/jeune |
| 6 | menos | weniger | less | moins |
| 18 | mentir | lügen | to lie | mentir |
| 13 | mercado, el | Markt, der | market | le marché |
| 19 | merecer la pena | sich lohnen | to be worth | valoir la peine |
| 4 | mesa, la | Tisch, der | table | la table |
| 8 | mes, el | Monat, der | month | le mois |
| 17 | meta, la | Ziel, das | finishing line; goal, objective | la ligne d'arrivée; le but; l'objectif |
| 14 | metro, el | U-bahn, die | Underground | le métro |
| 5 | mi | mein, meine, mein | my | mon; ma |
| 22 | miedo, el | Angst, die | fear, dread | la peur |
| 14 | mientras | während, währenddessen | while; as long as | pendant que; tant que |
| 22 | mientras tanto | inzwischen, währenddessen | meanwhile | entre-temps; pendant ce temps |
| 3 | miércoles, el | Mittwoch, der | Wednesday | mercredi |
| 6 | mil | tausend | thousand | mille |

| UNIDAD | ESPAÑOL | ALEMÁN | INGLÉS | FRANCÉS |
|---|---|---|---|---|
| 15 | millonario, el | Millionär, der | millionaire | le millionnaire |
| 6 | millón, el | Million, die | million | million |
| 6 | mineral | mineral… | mineral | minéral |
| 22 | mínimo, como | mindestens | at the very least | au minimun |
| 18 | ministro, el | Minister, der | minister | le ministre |
| 6 | minuto, el | Minute, die | minute | la minute |
| 10 | mío | meiner, meins | mine | le mien; à moi |
| 7 | mirar | schauen; sehen | to look | regarder |
| 20 | misa, la | Messe, die | mass | la messe |
| 15 | mismo, el/la/lo | der/die/dasselbe | the same | le/la même |
| 8 | mixto | gemischt | mixed | mixte |
| 13 | modelo, el | Modell, das | model | le modèle |
| 3 | moderno | modern | modern | moderne |
| 23 | mojado | naß | wet; damp | mouillé |
| 9 | mojar | naß machen | to wet; to damp | mouiller |
| 11 | molestar | stören | to annoy; to bother | gêner; déranger |
| 13 | molestia, la | Mühe, die | nuisance | le dérangement |
| 20 | momento, el | Augenblick; Moment, der | moment | le moment |
| 17 | monasterio, el | Kloster, das | monastery | le monastère |
| 9 | montaña, la | Berg, der | mountain | la montagne |
| 18 | monte, el | Berg, der | mountain; hill | le mont |
| 17 | monumento, el | (Bau) Denkmal, das | monument | le monument |
| 8 | morder | beißen | to bite | mordre |
| 2 | moreno | schwarzhaarig | brown | brun |
| 9 | morir(se) | sterben | to die | mourir |
| 7 | mostrar | zeigen | to show | montrer |
| 22 | motivo, el | Grund, der | motive | le motif |
| 19 | motor, el | Motor, der | engine | le moteur |
| 23 | mover | bewegen | to move | remuer; mouvoir déplacer |
| 19 | muchas gracias | vielen Dank! | thank you very much! | merci beaucoup! |
| 5 | mucho | viel | much; a lot of | beaucoup de |
| 1 | mucho gusto | sehr erfreut, freut mich | nice to meet you | enchanté |
| 4 | mueble, el | Möbel, das | piece of furniture | le meuble |
| 5 | mujer, la | Frau, die | woman | la femme |
| 10 | multinacional | multinational | multinational | multinational |
| 15 | mundo, el | Welt, die | world | le monde |
| 8 | muñeca, la | Puppe, die | doll | la poupée |
| 3 | museo, el | Museum, das | museum | le musée |
| 11 | música, la | Musik, die | music | la musique |
| 19 | músico, el | Musiker, der | musician | le musicien |
| 2 | muy | sehr | very | trés |

# N

| UNIDAD | ESPAÑOL | ALEMÁN | INGLÉS | FRANCÉS |
|---|---|---|---|---|
| 20 | nacer | geboren werden | to be born | naître |
| 6 | nacimiento, el | Geburt, die | birth | la naissance |
|  | nacional | national | national | national |
| 8 | nación, la | Nation, die | nation | la nation |
| 11 | nada | nichts | nothing | rien |
| 9 | nadar | schwimmen | to swim | nager |
| 11 | nadie | niemand | nobody | personne |
| 6 | naranja, la | Apfelsine, die | orange | l'orange |
| 17 | natal | Geburts… | natal; … of birth | natal |
| 19 | Navidad, la | Weihnacht, die | Christmas | le Noël |
| 23 | necesario | nötig | necessary | nécessaire |
| 7 | necesitar | brauchen | to need | avoir besoin de; nécessiter |
| 7 | negar | verneinen | to deny | nier |
| 5 | negro | schwarz | black | noir |
| 21 | nervio, el | Nerv, der | nerve | le nerf |
| 4 | nervioso | nervös | nervous | nerveux |
| 6 | nevar | schneien | to snow | neiger |
| 11 | nevera, la | Kühlschrank, der | refrigerator | le réfrigérateur |
| 22 | ni | weder… noch | neither; nor | ni |
| 2 | nicaragüense | nicaraguanisch; Nicaraguaner, der | Nicaraguan | Nicaraguayen |
| 6 | niebla, la | Nebel, der | fog; heavy mist | le brouillard |
| 5 | nieto, el | Enkel, der | grandson; grandchild | le petit-fils |
| 6 | nieve, la | Schnee, der | snow | la neige |
| 11 | ningún | kein | any; no | aucun |
| 11 | ninguno | keiner | none; anybody | aucun |

| UNIDAD | ESPAÑOL | ALEMÁN | INGLÉS | FRANCÉS |
|---|---|---|---|---|
| 15 | niñez, la | Kindheit, die | childhood | l'enfance |
| 2 | niño, el | Kind, das | child | l'enfant |
| 7 | nivel, el | Niveau, das | level | le niveau |
| 1 | no | Nein; nicht | no; not | non |
| 1 | ¡no importa! | das macht nichts! ¡keine Ursache! | doesn't matter! | C'est pas grave! |
| 6 | noche, la | Nacht, die | night | la nuit |
| 6 | norte, el | Norden, der | north | le nord |
| 2 | norteamericano | nordamerikanisch; Nordamerikaner, der | North American | Nord-americain |
| 2 | noruego | norwegisch; Norweger, der | Norwegian | Norvégien |
| 1 | nosotros | wir | we | nous |
| 19 | nota, la | Note, die | note | la note |
| 11 | notable | gut; befriedigend | second class mark | la dictinction/bien bien |
| 7 | noticia, la | Nachricht, die | a piece of news | la nouvelle |
| 6 | novecientos | neunhundert | nine hundred | neuf cents |
| 15 | novela, la | Roman, der | novel | le roman |
| 13 | noveno | neunt… | ninth | neuvième |
| 4 | noventa | neunzig | ninety | quatre-vingt-dix |
| 6 | noviembre | November, der | November | Novembre |
| 5 | novio, el | Freund, der | groom; boyfriend | le fiancé; le petit ami |
| 6 | nube, la | Wolke, die | cloud | le nuage |
| 6 | nublado | bewölkt | cloudy | nuageux |
| 20 | nublarse | sich bewölken | to cloud over | s'assombrir; se couvrir de nuages |
| 2 | nuestro | unser | our | notre |
| 1 | nueve | neun | nine | neuf |
| 4 | nuevo | neu | new | nouveau; nouvel |
| 23 | Nuevo Año, el | Neujahr, das | New year | le Nouvel an |
| 5 | número, el | Nummer, die | number | le numéro |
| 20 | numeroso | zahlreich | numerous; many | nombreux |
| 11 | nunca | nie | never | jamais |

# O

| UNIDAD | ESPAÑOL | ALEMÁN | INGLÉS | FRANCÉS |
|---|---|---|---|---|
| 10 | obedecer | gehorchen | to obey | obéir à |
| 19 | objeto, el | Gegenstand, der; Sache, die | object | l'object |
| 23 | obligar | verpflichten | to force; to oblige | obliger |
| 11 | obra, la | Werk, das | work | l'oeuvre; le travail |
| 16 | obrero, el | Arbeiter, der | worker | l'ouvrier |
| 23 | ocasión, la | Gelegenheit, die | occasion | l'occasion |
| 11 | ocio, el | Freizeitbeschäftigung, die | leisure | le loisir |
| 13 | octavo | acht… | eighth | huitième |
| 6 | octubre | Oktober, der | October | Octobre |
| 4 | ocupado | besetzt | busy | occupé |
| 21 | ocupar(se) | einnehmen | to occupy | occuper |
| 16 | ocurrir | geschehen | to happen; to occur | arriver; se passer |
| 4 | ochenta | achtzig | eighty | quatre-vingts |
| 1 | ocho | acht | eight | huit |
| 6 | ochocientos | achthundert | eight hundred | huit cents |
| 16 | oeste, el | Westen, der | west | l'ouest |
| 13 | oferta, la | Angebot, das | offer; special offer | l'offre |
| 21 | oficial | Amts…; offiziell | official | officiel |
| 3 | oficina, la | Büro, das | office | le bureau |
| 10 | ofrecer | anbieten | to offer | offrir |
| 9 | oír | hören | to hear | entendre |
| 23 | ¡ojalá! | hoffentlich! | if only…! | pourvu que…! |
| 8 | ojo, el | Auge, das | eye | l'oeil |
| 8 | oler | riechen | to smell | sentir |
| 8 | olor, el | Geruch, der | smell | l'odeur |
| 1 | once | elf | eleven | onze |

| UNIDAD | ESPAÑOL | ALEMÁN | INGLÉS | FRANCÉS |
|---|---|---|---|---|
|  | ópera, la | Oper, die | opera | l'opéra |
| 19 | oposición, la | staatliche Auswahlprüfung, die | public competitive examination | le concours |
| 4 | ordenado | ordentlich | tidy; orderly | ordonné |
| 23 | ordenar | befehlen | to order; to command | ordonner |
| 16 | oriental | orientalisch | eastern; oriental | oriental |
| 4 | origen, el | Herkunft, die | origin | l'origine |
| 21 | orilla, la | Ufer, das | shore; bank | la rive; le bord |
| 19 | oro, el | Gold, das | gold | l'or |
| 15 | orquesta, la | Orchester, das | orchestra | l'orchestre |
| 19 | oscuro | dunkel | dark; obscure | obscur |
| 6 | otoño, el | Herbst, der | autumn | l'automne |
| 17 | otro | noch ein(er /s) | other | autre |

## P

| UNIDAD | ESPAÑOL | ALEMÁN | INGLÉS | FRANCÉS |
|---|---|---|---|---|
| 12 | paciencia, la | Geduld, die | patience | la patience |
| 5 | padre, el | Vater, der | father | le père |
| 8 | paella, la | Paella, die | paella (spanish dish with rice cooked in the Valencian way) | la paëlla (le riz à la valencienne) |
| 14 | pagar | (be)zahlen | to pay | payer |
| 22 | pago, el | Zahlung, die | payment | le paiement |
| 17 | paisaje, el | Landschaft, die | landscape | le paysage |
| 5 | país, el | Land, das | country; nation | le pays |
| 15 | pájaro, el | Vogel, der | bird | l'oiseau |
| 17 | palacio, el | Palast, der | palace | le palais |
| 11 | pan, el | Brot, das | bread | le pain |
| 17 | panorama, el | Panorama, das | panorama; view | la panorama |
| 5 | pantalón, el | Hose, die | trousers | le pantalon |
| 17 | panteón, el | Gruft, die | pantheon | le panthéon |
| 4 | papelera, la | Papierkorb, der | waste paper basket | le corbeille à papier |
| 9 | paquete, el | Paket, das | packet; parcel | le paquet |
| 5 | para | für | for; to; in order to | pour; vers |
| 4 | parada, la | Haltestelle, die | stop | l'arrêt |
| 17 | parador, el | Parador, der (staatliches Hotel) | stateowned hotel | le parador; l'hôtel administrés par l'Etat |
| 5 | paraguas, el | Regenschirm, der | umbrella | le parapluie |
| 11 | paralizar | einstellen | to paralyze | paralyser |
| 21 | parcela, la | Grundstück, das | plot of land; smallholding | la parcelle |
| 11 | parecer | finden; gefallen | to seem; to appear | sembler; paraître |
| 7 | pared, la | Wand, die | wall | le mur |
| 22 | pariente, el | Verwandte, der | relative | le parent |

| UNIDAD | ESPAÑOL | ALEMÁN | INGLÉS | FRANCÉS |
|---|---|---|---|---|
| 16 | paro, el | Streik, der | strike | le chômage |
| 5 | parque, el | Park, der | park | le parc |
| 5 | parque de atracciones, el | Vergnügungspark, der | fair ground | |
| 6 | parte del día, la | Tageszeit, die | part of of the day | la partie du jour |
| 22 | parte, la | Teil, der | part | la partie |
| 21 | particular, un | Privatperson, eine | private individual | un particulier |
| 7 | partido, el | Spiel, das | match | la partie; le match |
| 9 | partir | teilen; abfahren | to divide; to leave; to set off | diviser; partir |
| 6 | pasado mañana | übermorgen | the day after tomorrow | après-demain |
| 14 | pasajero, el | Passagier, der | passenger | le passager |
| 14 | pasaporte, el | Reisepaß, der | passport | le passport |
| 10 | pasar | verbringen | to happen | passer |
| 20 | pasar por | vorbeigehen an | to pass through | passer pour |
| 17 | pasar la noche | übernachten | to spend the night | passer la nuit |
| 15 | pasarlo bien | sich amüsieren | to enjoy oneself | s'amuser |
| 7 | pasear | spazieren | to go for a walk | promener |
| 15 | paseo, el | Spaziergang, der | walk | la balade; le tour |
| 4 | pasillo, el | Korridor, der | corridor | le couloir |
| 7 | paso de cebra, el | Zebrastreifen, der | zebra crossing | le passage pour piétons |
| 6 | pastel, el | Kuchen, der | cake | le gâteau |
| 12 | pastilla, la | Tablette, die | tablet | le cachet |
| | pata, la | Bein, das | foot; leg (furniture) | la patte; le pied (du meuble) |
| 6 | patata, la | Kartoffel, die | potato | la pomme de terre |
| 7 | pausa, la | Pause, die | pause | la pause |
| | paz, la | Friede, der | peace | la paix |
| 9 | pedir | bitten | to ask for | demander |
| 16 | pegarse un susto | erschrecken | to frighten | avoir une peur bleue |
| 9 | peinar(se) | (sich) kämmen | to comb one's hair | se coiffer; se peigner |
| 6 | película, la | Film, der | film | le film |
| 9 | peligro, el | Gefahr, die | danger | lo póril |
| 17 | peligroso | gefährlich | dangerous | dangereux |
| 9 | pelo, el | Haar, das | hair | le cheveux; le poil |
| 18 | pelota, la | Ball, der | ball | la balle |
| 12 | peluquería, la | Frisiersalon, der | hairdresser's; barber's | le salon de coiffure |
| 1 | peluquero, el | Friseur, der | hairdresser | le coiffeur |
| 21 | pena, la | Leid, das | pity; sadness | la peine |
| 7 | pensar | denken | to think | penser |
| 5 | pensión, la | Pension, die | pension; guest house | la pension |
| | peor | schlimmer | worse | pire |
| 19 | peor, lo | Schlimmste, das | the worst | le pire |

| UNIDAD | ESPAÑOL | ALEMÁN | INGLÉS | FRANCÉS |
|---|---|---|---|---|
| 2 | pequeño | klein | little; small | petit |
| 6 | pera, la | Birne, die | pear | la poire |
| 13 | perchero, el | Haken, der | hallstand | le portemanteau |
| 8 | perder | verlieren | to lose | perdre |
| 18 | perder el tren | den Zug verpassen | to miss the train | rater le train |
| 18 | perderse | sich verirren; verlaufen | to get lost | se perdre |
| 13 | perdonar | verzeihen | to forgive | pardonner |
| 22 | perfección, la | Vollkommenheit, die | perfection | la perfection |
| 16 | perfume, el | Parfüm, das | perfume; scent | le parfum |
| 4 | periódico, el | Zeitung, die | newspaper | le journal |
| 17 | periodista, el/la | Journalist, der/-in, die | journaist | le journaliste |
| 19 | perla, la | Perle, die | pearl | la perle |
| 20 | permanecer | bleiben | to stay; to remain | rester |
| 23 | permitir | erlauben | to allow; to permit | permettre |
| 4 | pero | aber | but | mais |
| 5 | perro, el | Hund, der | dog | le chien |
| 5 | persona, la | Person, die | person | la personne |
| 2 | peruano | peruanisch; Peruaner, der | Peruvian | Péruvien |
| 5 | pesar | wiegen | to weigh | peser |
| 16 | pescado, el | Fisch, der | fish | le poisson |
| 15 | pescar | fischen | to fish | pêcher |
| 5 | peseta, la | Pesete, die | peseta | la peseta |
| 6 | peso, el | Peso, der | weight | le poids |
| 15 | pez, el | Fisch, der | fish | le poisson |
| 7 | piano, el | Klavier, das | piano | le piano |
| 20 | pictórico | malerisch | pictorical | pictural |
| 16 | piedra, la | Stein, der | stone | la pierre |
| 19 | pie, el | Fuß, der | foot | le pied |
| 11 | piel, la | Haut, die | skin | la peau |
| 16 | pierna, la | Bein, das | leg | la jambe |
| 21 | pieza, la | Stück, das | piece | la pièce |
| 1 | piloto, el | Pilot, der | pilot | le pilote |
| 7 | pintar | malen | to paint | peindre |
| 20 | pintor, el | Maler, der | painter | le peintre |
| 17 | pintura, la | Malerei, die | paint | la peinture |
| 15 | pipa, la | Pfeife, die | pipe | la pipe |
| 14 | pisar | treten | to step on | marcher sur |
| 4 | piscina, la | Schwimmbad, das | swimming pool | la piscine |
| 13 | piso, el | Stockwerk, das | flat | l'appartement |
| 19 | pista, la | Spur, die | clue | la piste |
| 22 | pizarra, la | Tafel, die | blackboard | le tableau |
| 11 | planchar | bügeln | to iron | repasser |
| 19 | planear | planen | to plan | faire le plan/ avoir en projet |
| 11 | plan, el | Plan, der | plan | le plan |

| UNIDAD | ESPAÑOL | ALEMÁN | INGLÉS | FRANCÉS |
|---|---|---|---|---|
| 9 | plano, el | Plan, der; Zeichnung, die | plan | le plan |
| 10 | planta, la | Etage, die; | floor | l'étage |
| 16 | plantilla, la | Belegschaft, die | staff | le personnel |
| 20 | plata, la | Silber, das | silver | l'argent |
| 6 | plátano, el | Banane, die | banana | la banane |
| 7 | plato, el | Teller, der | plate | l'assiette |
| 5 | playa, la | Strand, der | beach | la plage |
| 3 | plaza, la | Platz, der | square | la place |
| 8 | pluma, la | Feder, die | feather | la plume |
| 3 | pobre | arm | poor | pauvre |
| 3 | poco | wenig | little | peu |
| 8 | poder | können | can | pouvoir |
| 22 | poema, el | Gedicht, das | poem | le poème |
|  | poeta, el | Dichter, der | poet | le poète |
| 2 | polaco | polnisch; Pole, der | Polish | Polonais |
| 7 | policía, la | Polizei, die | police | la police |
| 18 | política, la | Politik, die | politics | la politique |
| 10 | político | politisch | political | politique |
| 19 | póliza, la | Police, die | tax stamp | la police |
| 18 | poner la mesa | den Tisch decken | to lay the table | mettre la table |
| 15 | ponerse de acuerdo | sich einigen | to come to an agreement | se mettre/tomber d'accord |
| 22 | ponerse de pie | aufstehen | to stand up | se mettre debout |
| 17 | ponerse en carretera | mit dem Auto abreisen | to set off by car | partir en voiture |
| 12 | popular | populär | popular | populaire |
| 16 | póquer, el | Pokerspiel, das | poker | le pòquer |
| 8 | por | durch | for; by; because of | pour; par |
| 4 | porcelana, la | Porzellan, das | china | la porcelaine |
| 13 | por desgracia | leider | unfortunately | malheureusement |
| 14 | por eso | deshalb | that is why... | à cause de ça |
| 6 | por favor | bitte | please | s'il vous plaît |
| 9 | por lo general | gewöhnlich | generally | généralement |
| 7 | ¿por qué? | warum? | why? | pourquoi? |
| 11 | por supuesto | selbstverständlich | of course | bien sûr |
| 2 | portugués | portugiesisch; Portugiese, der | Portuguese | Portugais |
| 23 | posibilidad, la | Möglichkeit, die | possibility | la possibilité |
| 12 | posible | möglich | possible | possible |
| 22 | posiblemente | möglich | possibly | possiblement |
| 23 | positivo | positiv | positive | positif |
| 18 | postal, la | Postkarte, die | postcard | la carte postale |
| 8 | postre, el | Nachtisch, der | dessert | le dessert |
| 13 | potente | leistungsfähig | powerful | puissant |
| 23 | prácticamente | praktisch | practically | pratiquement |

| UNIDAD | ESPAÑOL | ALEMÁN | INGLÉS | FRANCÉS |
|---|---|---|---|---|
| 7 | practicar | üben | to practise | pratiquer |
| 13 | precio, el | Preis, der | price | le prix |
| 9 | preferir | vorziehen | to prefer | préférer |
| 7 | preguntar | fragen | to ask | demander |
| 18 | premio, el | Preis, der | prize; reward | la récompense |
| 15 | prensa, la | Presse, die | press | la presse |
| 12 | preocupado | besorgt | worried | préoccupé |
| 9 | preocuparse de/por | sorgen für/um | to worry about | se préoccuper |
| 9 | preparar | vorbereiten | to prepare | préparer |
| 20 | prepararse para | sich vorbereiten für | to get ready for | se préparer à |
| 10 | presentar(se) | (sich) vorstellen | to introduce oneself | se présenter |
| 17 | presidente, el | Präsident, der | president | le président |
| 8 | prestar | leihen | to lend | prêter |
| 6 | primavera, la | Frühling, der | spring | le printemps |
| 17 | primer | erst… | first | le premier |
| 8 | primero, de | zuerst; als erster Gang | for a start | d'entrée |
| 5 | primo, el | Cousin, der | cousin | le cousin |
| 16 | principio, el | Anfang; Beginn, der | beginning; start | le commencement; le début |
| 13 | prisa, la | Eile, die | urgency/hurry | l'hâte |
| 23 | privado | privat | private | privé |
| 23 | probable | wahrscheinlich | probable | probable |
| 11 | probar(se) | anprobieren | to try (on) | essayer |
| 3 | problema, el | Problem, das | problem | le problème |
| 10 | producir | herstellen | to produce | produire |
| 7 | producto, el | Produkt, das | product | le produit |
| 23 | profesional | Berufs… | professional | professionnel |
| 4 | profesión, la | Beruf, der | profession; career | la profession |
| 1 | profesor, el | Lehrer; Professor, der | teacher; professor; lecturer | le professeur |
| 12 | profundamente | tief | deeply | profondément |
| 22 | programar | programmieren | to programme | programmer |
| 20 | prohibir | verbieten | to forbid | interdire |
| 19 | prometer | versprechen | to promise | promettre |
| 4 | pronto | bald | soon | prompt; rapide |
| 18 | propaganda | Werbung, die | propaganda | la propagande |
| 11 | proponer | vorschlagen | to propose | proposer |
| 22 | prospecto, el | Prospekt, der | prospectus | le prospectus |
| 23 | próspero | glücklich | prosperous | prospère |
| 21 | protección, la | Unterstützung, die | protection | la protection |
| 16 | protesta, la | Protest, der | protest | la protestation |
| 3 | provincial | Provinz… | provincial | provincial |
| 8 | próximo | nächst… | next | prochaine |
| 13 | proyecto, el | Projekt, das | project | le project |

| UNIDAD | ESPAÑOL | ALEMÁN | INGLÉS | FRANCÉS |
|---|---|---|---|---|
| 18 | publicar | veröffentlichen | to publish; to make public | publier |
| 18 | público | öffentlich | public | public |
| 4 | pueblo, el | Dorf, das | village; country town | le village;/la petite ville |
| 21 | puente, el | Brücke, die | bridge | le pont |
| 7 | puerta, la | Tür, die | door | la porte |
| 16 | puerto, el | Hafen, der | port | le port |
| 2 | puertorriqueño | Puertoricaner, der | Puerto Rican | le Portoricain |
| 4 | pues | denn | then; so; well | puisque |
| 13 | puesto, el | Stelle, die | post | la situation; le poste |
| 20 | pulsera, la | Armband, das | bracelet | le bracelet |
| 12 | pulso, el | Puls, der | pulse | le pouls |
| 11 | puntual | pünktlich | punctual | ponctuel |
| 13 | puro, el | Zigarre, die | cigar | le cigare |

## Q

| UNIDAD | ESPAÑOL | ALEMÁN | INGLÉS | FRANCÉS |
|---|---|---|---|---|
| 1 | ¿qué? | was? | what? | Quoi? |
| 6 | ¿qué hora es? | wieviel Uhr/ wie spät ist es? | what time is it? | Quelle heure est-il? |
| 6 | ¡qué mala pata! | was für ein Pech! | How unlucky! What bad luck! | avoir la poisse/ la guigne |
| 9 | quedar(se) | bleiben | to stay | rester |
| 8 | querer | möchten | to want | vouloir |
| 11 | queso, el | Käse, der | cheese | le fromage |
| 1 | ¿quién? | wer? | who? | qui? |
| 1 | quince | fünfzehn | fifteen | quinze |
| 23 | quiniela, la | Fußballtoto, das | pools coupon | les mutuels |
| 13 | quinto | fünft… | fifth | cinquième |
|  | quiosco, el | Kiosk, der | kiosk | le kiosque |
| 9 | quitar(se) | (sich) ausziehen | to take off; to take away | s'enlever |
| 18 | quitar la mesa | den Tisch abdecken | to clean the table | débarrasser la table |

# R

| UNIDAD | ESPAÑOL | ALEMÁN | INGLÉS | FRANCÉS |
|---|---|---|---|---|
| 6 | ración, la | Portion, die | portion | la portion |
| 17 | radiador, el | Kühler, der | radiator | le radiateur |
| 3 | radio, la | Radio, das | radio | la radio |
| 10 | rápidamente | schnell | fast | rapidement |
| 22 | rapidez, la | Schnelligkeit, die | quickness; speed | la rapidité |
| 3 | rápido | schnell | fast; quick | rapide |
| 11 | rato, hasta dentro de un | bis gleich! | I'll see you later/soon! | à bientôt! |
| 22 | realidad, la | Wirklichkeit, die | reality | la realité |
| 13 | rebaja, la | Ausverkauf, der | price reduction | la réduction |
| 13 | rebajado | herabgesetzt | reduced | rabaissé |
| 12 | recetar | verschreiben | to prescribe | ordonner; prescrire |
| 9 | recibir | empfangen | to receive | recevoir |
| 20 | recital, el | (Solo) konzert, das | recital | le récital |
| 14 | recoger | abholen | to get;to fetch | prendre |
| 8 | recomendar | empfehlen | to recommend | recommander |
| 7 | recordar | erinnern | to remember; to recall | rappeler |
| 15 | recuerdo, el | Erinnerung, die | memory | le souvenir |
| 4 | redondo | rund | round | rond |
| 17 | reducir(se) | (sich) beschränken | to be reduced to | se réduire |
| 15 | refugio de montaña, el | Schutzhütte, die | mountain hut | le refuge à la montagne |
| 8 | regalar | schenken | to make a present to s. o. | offrir |
| 8 | regalo, el | Geschenk, das | present | le cadeau |
| 21 | regar | (be) gießen | to water | arroser |
| 19 | región, la | Gegend, die | region | la région |
| 14 | regresar | zurückkehren | to come back | revenir |

| UNIDAD | ESPAÑOL | ALEMÁN | INGLÉS | FRANCÉS |
|---|---|---|---|---|
| 9 | reír(se) de | sich über etwas/ jmdn lustig machen | to laugh at | rire de |
| 12 | relajarse | sich entspannen | to relax | se relâcher; se relaxer |
| 4 | reloj, el | Uhr, die | watch; clock | l'horloge |
| 18 | rellenar | ausfüllen | to fill up | remplir |
| 19 | renovar | renovieren | to renew | renouveler |
| 11 | renunciar | verzichten | to renounce; to give up | renoncer; abandonner |
| 14 | reparar | reparieren | to repair; to mend | réparer |
| 7 | repasar | nachsehen; überprüfen | to revise; to re-examine | repasser; revoir |
| 9 | repetir(se) | (sich) wiederholen | to recur | se répéter; revenir |
| 15 | representar | darstellen | to represent | représenter |
| 22 | reserva, la | Vorbestellung, die | reserve; reservation | la réserve; la réservation |
| 11 | reservar | reservieren | to reserve | réserver |
| 4 | resfriado, el | Erkältung, die | cold | le rhum |
| 17 | resolver | lösen | to solve | résoudre |
| 12 | respirar | atmen | to breath | respirer |
| 22 | responder | antworten | to answer | répondre |
| 5 | restaurante, el | Restaurant, das | restaurant | le restaurant |
| 21 | resultado, el | Ergebnis, das | result | le résultat |
| 20 | resultar + adj. | werden + adj. | to turn out; to be + adj. | être + adj. |
|  | resumen, el | Zusammenfassung, die | summary | le résumé |
| 18 | retirado | abseits gelegen; entfernt | remoted | retiré |
| 22 | retrasar(se) | (sich) verspäten | to be late | (se) retarder; (s') attarder |
| 16 | retraso, el | Verspätung, die | delay | le retard |
| 18 | reunir(se) | (sich) versammeln | to meet; to assemble | (se) réunir |
| 14 | revisar | nachprüfen | to revise | réviser |
| 7 | revista, la | Illustrierte, die | magazine | la magazine |
| 19 | revolver | durcheinander bringen | to move about | remuer; fouiller dans |
| 19 | revuelto | durcheinander | in disorder | mis sens dessus dessous |
| 17 | rey, el | König, der | king | le roi |
| 3 | rico | reich | rich | riche |
| 8 | rincón, el | Ecke, die | corner | le coin |
| 12 | río, el | Fluß, der | river | le fleuve |
| 19 | robar | einbrechen; stehlen | to rob; to steal | voler |
| 19 | robo, el | Einbruch; Diebstahl, der | theft; robbery | le vol |
| 15 | rocoso | felsig | rocky | rocheux |
| 17 | rodear | umgeben | to surround | entourer |
| 7 | rogar | bitten | to plead with; to beg | supplier; prier |
| 5 | rojo | rot | red | rouge |
| 3 | románico | romanisch | romanesque; romanic | roman |

| UNIDAD | ESPAÑOL | ALEMÁN | INGLÉS | FRANCÉS |
|---|---|---|---|---|
| 17 | romano | römisch | Roman | romain |
| 18 | romper | kaputt machen; zerbrechen | to break | casser |
| 8 | ropa, la | Kleidung, die | clothes | le vêtement |
| 9 | rosa, la | Rose, die | rose | la rose |
| 3 | roto | kaputt | broken | cassé |
| 2 | rubio | blond | blonde | blond |
| 6 | rublo, el | Rubel, der | rouble | le rouble |
| 11 | ruido, el | Lärm, der | noise | le bruit |
| 23 | ruidoso | lärmend; laut | noisy | bruyant |
| 2 | ruso | Russisch; Russe, der | Russian | Russe |
| 7 | ruta, la | (Reise) Weg, der | route | la route |

# S

| UNIDAD | ESPAÑOL | ALEMÁN | INGLÉS | FRANCÉS |
|---|---|---|---|---|
| 6 | sábado, el | Samstag, der | Saturday | le samedi |
| 8 | saber | wissen | to know | savoir |
| 13 | sabor, el | Geschmack, der | taste | le goût |
| 12 | sacar dinero | Geld abheben | to draw out money | retirer de l'argent |
| 12 | sacar una entrada | eine Eintrittskarte kaufen | to get the ticket | prendre un billet |
| 6 | salado | salzig | salty | salé |
| 5 | sala, la | Saal, der | room; hall | la salle |
| 13 | salida, la | Abflug, der | departure | le départ |
| 9 | salir | abfahren; ausgehen | to go out | sortir/partir |
| 20 | salir de viaje | abreisen | to set off | partir en voyage |
| 4 | salón-comedor, el | Wohn-Eßzimmer, das | living/dinning room | la salle à manger |
| 4 | saludar | (be)grüßen | to greet | saluer |
| 21 | salud, la | Gesundheit, die | health | la santé |
| 23 | salvar(se) | (sich) retten | to save (s. o.) | sauver |
| 20 | sangría, la | Rotweinbowle, die | sangria; drink with sugar, red wine, lemon, orange... | la sangria; boisson sucrée à base de vin rouge et de jus de citron |
| 9 | secar(se) | (sich) abtrocknen | to dry off | se sécher |
| 6 | seco | trocken | dry | sec |
| 1 | secretaria, la | Sekretärin, die | secretary | la secrétaire |
| 13 | sed, la | Durst, der | thirst | la soif |
| 12 | seguir una dieta | Diät halten | to be on a diet | être à la diéte/au régime |
| 17 | según | nach | according to | selon |

| UNIDAD | ESPAÑOL | ALEMÁN | INGLÉS | FRANCÉS |
|---|---|---|---|---|
| 8 | segundo, de | als Hauptgericht | secondly | deuxièmement |
| 6 | segundo, el | Sekunde, die | second | le plat principal |
| 19 | seguramente | sicher | for sure; surely | sûrement |
| 16 | seguridad, la | Sicherheit, die | security, safety | la securité |
| 14 | seguro | sicher | sure | sûr |
| 19 | seguro, el | Versicherung, die | insurance | l'assurance |
| 1 | seis | sechs | six | six |
| 6 | seiscientos | sechshundert | six hundred | six cents |
| 20 | seleccionar | auswählen | to choose | sélectionner |
| 6 | semana, la | Woche, die | week | la semaine |
| 7 | sentar(se) | (sich) setzen | to sit down | (s') asseoir |
| 9 | sentir | fühlen | to feel | sentir |
| 16 | señal, la | Zeichen, das | sign | le signal |
| 3 | señor, el | Herr, der | sir; Mr | le monsieur |
| 3 | señora, la | Frau, die | lady; Mrs | la dame |
| 3 | señorita, la | Fräulein, das | young lady; Miss | la jeune fille; mademoiselle |
| 5 | separado | getrennt | separated | séparé |
| 6 | septiembre | September, der | September | le septembre |
| 13 | séptimo | siebt… | seventh | septième |
| 1 | ser | sein | to be | être |
| 19 | serio | ernst | serious | sérieux |
| 4 | servicios, los | Toiletten, die | toilets | les toilettes |
| 9 | servir | servieren | to serve | servir |
| 22 | servir a alguien en algo | jmdm bei etwas behilflich sein | to help someone doing something | rendre service à quelqu'un |
| 3 | sesenta | sechzig | sixty | soixante |
| 6 | setecientos | siebenhundert | seven hundred | sept cents |
| 4 | setenta | siebzig | seventy | soixante dix |
| 13 | sexto | sechst… | sixth | sixième |
| 12 | si | wenn | if; whether | si |
| 6 | siempre | immer | always | toujours |
| 16 | sierra, la | Gebirge, das | mountain range | la chaîne de montagnes |
| 9 | siesta, la | Siesta, die | siesta; nap | la sieste |
| 1 | siete | sieben | seven | sept |
| 3 | siglo, el | Jahrhundert, das | century | le siècle |
| 17 | siguiente | (nach) folgend | following; next | suivant |
| 20 | silencio, el | Schweigen, das | silence | le silence |
| 4 | silla, la | Stuhl, der | chair | la chaise |
| 4 | sillón, el | Sessel, der | armchair | le fauteuil |
| 2 | simpático | sympathisch | nice | sympathique |
| 19 | sin duda | zweifellos | of course! | sans doute |
| 18 | sinceramente | ehrlich | sincerely | sincèrement |
| 20 | sin embargo | trotzdem | however | cependant |

| UNIDAD | ESPAÑOL | ALEMÁN | INGLÉS | FRANCÉS |
|---|---|---|---|---|
| 17 | sinfonía, la | Symphonie, die | symphony | la symphonie |
| 11 | sitio, el | Platz, der | place | la place |
| 4 | situación, la | Situation, die | situation | la situation |
| 17 | situado, estar | liegen | to be located/placed | être situé |
| 4 | sobre | auf; über | on; over; above | sur |
| 12 | sobre todo | besonders | above all | surtout |
| 19 | sobresaliente, el | sehr gut | first class mark | reçu avec mention; très bien |
| 5 | sobrino, el | Neffe, der | nephew | le neveu |
| 23 | sociedad, la | Gesellschaft, die | society | la société |
| 13 | sofá, el | Sofa, das | sofa | le sofa; le canapé |
| 16 | solamente | nur | only | seulement |
| 8 | soldado, el | Soldat, der | soldier | le soldat |
| 6 | sol, el | Sonne, die | sun | le soleil |
| 23 | solicitar | sich bewerben um | to apply | solliciter |
| 17 | solicitud, la | Bewerbungsschreiben, das | application | la demande |
| 20 | solista, el/la | Solist, der/-in, die | soloist | le soliste |
| 5 | solo | selbst | self | même |
| 16 | solo | allein | alone | seul |
| 5 | soltero | ledig | single | célibataire |
| 11 | solucionar | lösen | to solve | résoudre |
| 11 | solución, la | Lösung, die | solution | la solution |
| 5 | sombrero, el | Hut, der | hat | le chapeau |
| 7 | sonar | klingeln; klingen | to ring | sonner |
| 17 | soñado | Traum… | dreamt | rêvé |
| 7 | sopa, la | Suppe, die | soup | la soupe |
| 14 | soprano, el/la | Sopran, der; Sopranistin, die | soprano | le/la soprano |
| 23 | sordo | taub | deaf | sourd |
| 23 | sordomudo | taubstumm | deaf and dumb | sourd-muet |
| 5 | su | sein; ihr | his/her/its | son/sa |
| 6 | suave | mild | smooth;soft | doux |
| 9 | subir | steigen | to go up | monter |
| 12 | subirse a | einsteigen in | to get on | monter en/dans |
| 12 | subirse la manga | den Ärmel hochziehen | to roll up one's sleeves | remonter ses manches |
| 19 | suceder | geschehen | to happen | passer |
| 16 | suceso, el | Ereignis, das | event; incident | l' événement |
| 4 | sucio | schmutzig | dirty | sale |
| 22 | sucursal, la | Filiale, die | subsidiary | la succursale |
| 2 | sudamericano | südamerikanisch; Südamerikaner, der | South American | Sud-américain |
| 2 | sueco | schwedisch; Schwede, der | Swedish | Suédois |
| 5 | suegro, el | Schwiegervater, der | father-in-law | le beau-père |

| UNIDAD | ESPAÑOL | ALEMÁN | INGLÉS | FRANCÉS |
|---|---|---|---|---|
| 22 | sueldo, el | Gehalt, das | salary | le salaire |
| 4 | suelo, el | Boden, der | floor | le sol |
| 20 | sueño, el | Schlaf, der | dream | le sommeil |
| 9 | suerte, la | Glück, das | luck | le sort; la chance |
| 18 | sufrir | leiden | to suffer | souffrir de |
| 2 | suizo | schweizerisch; Schweizer, der | Swiss | Suisse |
| 23 | suplicar | bitten; flehen | to beg; to plead for | supplier |
| 19 | suponer | annehmen; voraussetzen | to suppose | supposer |
| 4 | sur, el | Süden, der | south | le sud |
| 18 | suspender | einstellen | to suspend | suspendre |
| 16 | susto, el | Schreck, der | fright; scare | la peur |
| 10 | suyo | seiner, seine seins; ihrer, ihre, ihrs | his/hers/theirs | à lui/à elle/à eux |

# T

| UNIDAD | ESPAÑOL | ALEMÁN | INGLÉS | FRANCÉS |
|---|---|---|---|---|
| 2 | tabaco, el | Tabak, der | tobacco | le tabac |
| 20 | taberna, la | Kneipe, die | tavern | la taverne |
| 20 | tablao, el | Bühne für; Flamenco, die | club of Flamenco | le cabaret andalou |
| 13 | tacón, el | Absatz, der | heel | le talon |
| 20 | taller, el | Werkstatt, die | workshop | l'atelier |
| 16 | tamaño, el | Größe, die | size | la taille |
| 3 | también | auch | also; too | aussi |
| 22 | tan | so | so; as; such | si; tant; aussi |
| 22 | tan sólo | nur | just | juste |
| 6 | tanto | so viel | so much | autant |
| 18 | taquilla, la | Kasse, die | ticket office | le guichet |
| 18 | tardar | brauchen; dauern | to take a long time | tarder |
| 6 | tarde, la | Nachmittag; Abend, der | afternoon; evening | l'après-midi le soir |
| 6 | tarta, la | Kuchen, der; Torte, die | cake | le gâteau |
| 16 | taxi, el | Taxi, das | taxi; cab | le taxi |
| 7 | taza, la | Tasse, die | cup | la tasse |
| 6 | teatro, el | Theater, das | theatre | le théâtre |
| 23 | telecomunicación, la | Fernmeldewesen, das | telecommunication | la télécommunication |
| 22 | telefonear | telefonieren | to telephone | téléphoner |
| 3 | teléfono, el | Telefon, das | telephone | le téléphone |
| 12 | telégrafo, el | Telegraph, der | telegraph | le télégraphe |
| 7 | telegrama, el | Telegramm, das | telegram | le télégramme |
| 8 | televisión, la | Fernsehen, das | television | la télévision |
| 4 | televisor, el | Fernseher, der | television set | le téléviseur |
| 21 | télex, el | Telex, das | telex | le télex |
| 3 | tema, el | Thema, das | subject; topic | le sujet |

| UNIDAD | ESPAÑOL | ALEMÁN | INGLÉS | FRANCÉS |
|---|---|---|---|---|
| 16 | temer(se) | fürchten | to be afraid | craindre |
| 6 | temperatura, la | Temperatur, die | temperature | la température |
| 6 | templado | mild | warm | tiède |
| 22 | temporada, la | Saison, die | season | la saison |
| 6 | temprano | früh | early | tôt |
| 8 | tender | aufhängen | to hang out | étendre le linge |
| 5 | tener | haben | to have | avoir |
| 13 | tener hambre | Hunger haben | to be hungry | avoir faim |
| 15 | tener lugar | stattfinden | to take place | avoir lieu |
| 13 | tener prisa | es eilig haben | to be in a hurry | avoir hâte de |
| 12 | tener que | müssen | to have to | devoir; falloir |
| 14 | tener razón | recht haben | to be right | avoir raison |
| 20 | tener sueño | schläfrig sein | to be sleepy | tomber de sommeil |
| 7 | tenis, el | Tennis (spiel), das | tennis | le tennis |
| 13 | tercero | dritt... | third | troisième |
| 10 | terminar | beenden | to finish | terminer; finir |
| 4 | terraza, la | Terrasse, die | terrace | la terrasse |
| 23 | tesis, la | Dissertation, die | thesis | la thèse |
| 18 | tesoro, el | Schatz, der | treasure | le trésor |
| 3 | textil | Textil... | textile | textile |
| 11 | texto, el | Text, der | text | le texte |
| 5 | tía, la | Tante, die | aunt | la tante |
| 4 | tiempo, el | Zeit, die | time | le temps |
| 5 | tienda, la | Laden, der; Geschäft, das | shop store | la boutique; le magasin |
| 6 | tierra, la | Erde, die | earth | la terre |
| 8 | tinto, el | Rotwein, der | red wine | le vin rouge |
| 5 | tío, el | Onkel, der | uncle | l' oncle |
| 20 | típico | typisch | typical | typique |
| 19 | tirar | werfen | to throw | jeter |
| 10 | toalla, la | Handtuch, das | towel | la serviette |
| 4 | tocadiscos, el | Plattenspieler, der | record player | le tourne-disque |
| 7 | tocar | spielen | to play | jouer |
| 20 | tocar la lotería | im Loto gewinnen | to win the pools | gagner à la loterie |
| 4 | todavía | noch | still; yet | encore |
| 9 | todo | alles | all | tout |
| 6 | tomar | nehmen | to take | prendre |
| 12 | tomar asiento | Platz nehmen | to take a seat | prendre un siège |
| 9 | tomar el sol | die Sonne nehmen | to sunbathe | s'exposer au soleil |
| 5 | tomate, el | Tomate, die | tomato | la tomate |
| 17 | tontería, la | Dummheit, die | nonsense | la sottise |
| 8 | torero, el | Stierkämpfer, der | bullfighter | le torero |
| 6 | tormenta, la | Gewitter, das | storm | l'orage |
| 20 | toro, el | Stier, der | bull | le taureau |
| 22 | torpeza, la | Ungeschicklichkeit, die | clumsiness | la maladresse |

| UNIDAD | ESPAÑOL | ALEMÁN | INGLÉS | FRANCÉS |
|---|---|---|---|---|
| 3 | torre, la | Turm, der | tour | la tour |
| 17 | torreón, el | Festungsturm, der | tower | la grosse tour |
| 12 | tortilla, la | Omelett, das | omelette | l'omelette |
| 14 | toser | husten | to cough | tousser |
| 22 | total | Gesamt… | total | total |
| 10 | trabajador | arbeitsam; | hard-working | travailleur |
| 16 | trabajador, el | Arbeiter, der | worker | le travailleur |
| 6 | trabajar | arbeiten | to work | travailler |
| 7 | trabajo, el | Arbeit, die | work | le travail |
| 10 | traducir | übersetzen | to translate | traduire |
| 8 | traer | bringen | to bring | apporter |
| 15 | tráfico, el | Verkehr, der | traffic | le trafic |
| 16 | traje, el | Anzug, der | suit | le costume |
| 11 | tranquilamente | ruhig | quietly | tranquillement |
| 16 | transporte, el | Transport, der | transport | le transport |
| 14 | transbordo, el | Umsteigen, das | change | le changement |
| 23 | trastada, la | üble Streich, der | mischief | la bêtise |
| 15 | tratar | behandeln | to treat | traiter |
| 23 | travieso | ausgelassen, unartig | mischievous | l'espiègle |
| 18 | trayecto, el | Fahrt; Strecke, die | journey | le trajet |
| 1 | trece | dreizehn | thirteen | treize |
| 2 | treinta | dreißig | thirty | trente |
| 9 | tren, el | Zug, der | train | le train |
| 1 | tres | drei | three | trois |
| 6 | trescientos | dreihundert | three hundred | trois cents |
| 6 | tres mil | dreitausend | three thousand | trois mille |
| 13 | trimestre, el | Vierteljahr, das | term | le trimestre |
| 23 | triste | traurig | sad | triste |
| 1 | tú | du | you | tu |
| 17 | tumba, la | Grab, das | grave | la tombe |
| 12 | tumbarse | sich hinlegen | to lie down | s'allonger |
| 16 | túnel, el | Tunnel, der | tunnel | le tunnel |
| 2 | turco | Türkisch; Türke, der | Turkish | Turc |
| 15 | turismo, el | Tourismus, der | tourism | le tourisme |
| 3 | turista, el | Tourist, der | tourist | le touriste |
| 4 | turístico | touristisch | tourist | touristique |
| 10 | tuyo | deiner, deins | yours | à toi |

## U

| UNIDAD | ESPAÑOL | ALEMÁN | INGLÉS | FRANCÉS |
| --- | --- | --- | --- | --- |
|  | último | letzt… | last | dernier |
| 3 | un | ein | a/an | un |
| 3 | una | eine | a/an | une |
| 13 | undécimo | elft… | eleventh | onzième |
| 23 | únicamente | nur | only | uniquement |
| 3 | único | einzig | only | unique |
|  | universidad, la | Universität, die | University | l'Université |
| 9 | uña, la | Nagel, der | nail | l'ongle |
| 22 | urgencia, la | Dringlichkeit, die | urgency | l' urgence |
| 23 | urgentemente | dringend; eilig | urgently | urgemment |
| 1 | usted/es | Sie | you (formal address) | vous |
| 21 | útil | nützlich | useful | utile |
| 6 | uva, la | (wein) traube, die | grape | le raisin |

## V

| UNIDAD | ESPAÑOL | ALEMÁN | INGLÉS | FRANCÉS |
| --- | --- | --- | --- | --- |
| 4 | vacaciones, las | Ferien, die; Urlaub, der | holidays | les vacances |
| 5 | vacío | leer | empty | vide |
| 6 | valer | kosten | to cost | valoir |
| 21 | valer la pena | sich lohnen | to be worth | valoir la peine |
| 19 | valorar | bewerten | to value | évaluer |
| 19 | valor, el | Wert, der | value | la valeur |
| 17 | valle, el | Tal, das | valley | la vallée |
| 17 | varios | einige; ein paar | several | plusieurs |
| 5 | vaso, el | Glas, das | glass | le verre |
| 16 | vecino, el | Nachbar, der | neighbour | le voisin |
| 16 | vehículo, el | Fahrzeug, das | vehicle | le véhicule |
| 1 | veinte | zwanzig | twenty | vingt |
| 8 | vendedor, el | Verkäufer, der | seller | le vendeur |
| 8 | vender | verkaufen | to sell | vendre |
| 2 | venezolano | venezolanisch; Venezolaner, der | Venezuelan | Vénézuélien |
| 8 | venir | kommen | to come | venir |
| 22 | venta, la | Verkauf, der | sale | la vente |
| 4 | ventana, la | Fenster, das | window | la fenêtre |
| 14 | ventanilla, la | Schalter, der | (small) window | le guichet |
| 8 | ver | sehen | to see | voir |
| 11 | veranear | den Sommer verbringen | to spend the summer holidays | passer les vacances d'été |
| 6 | verano, el | Sommer, der | summer | l' été |
| 6 | ¿verdad? | wirklich?; nicht wahr? | isn't it? (question tags) | n'est-ce pas? |
| 9 | verdad, la | Wahrheit, die | truth | la vérité |
| 5 | verde | grün | green | vert |

| UNIDAD | ESPAÑOL | ALEMÁN | INGLÉS | FRANCÉS |
|---|---|---|---|---|
| 4 | vestíbulo, el | Diele; Vorhalle, die | hall; lobby | le vestibule; le hall |
| 11 | vestido, el | Kleid, das | dress | la robe |
| 16 | vestido de noche, el | Abendkleid, das | evening dress | la robe du soir |
| 9 | vestir(se) | (sich) anziehen | to get dressed | s'habiller |
| 14 | viajar | reisen | to travel | voyager |
| 11 | viaje, el | Reise, die | travel; trip voyage | le voyage |
| 12 | vida, la | Leben, das | life | la vie |
| 4 | viejo | alt | old | vieux |
| 6 | viento, el | Wind, der | wind | le vent |
| 6 | viernes, el | Freitag, der | Friday | Vendredi |
| 4 | vietnamita | vietnamesisch; Vietnamese, der | Vietnamese | Vietnamien |
| 16 | vigilar | beobachten | to watch | surveiller |
| 2 | vino, el | Wein, der | wine | le vin |
| 11 | visita, la | Besuch, der | visit | la visite |
| 7 | visitar | besichtigen; besuchen | to visit | visiter |
| 22 | vista, la | Blick, der | sight | la vue |
| 5 | viudo | verwitwet; Witwer, der | widowed | veuf |
| 19 | vivienda, la | Wohnung, die | accommodation | le logement |
| 9 | vivir | leben; wohnen | to live | vivre |
| 7 | volar | fliegen | to fly | voler |
| 8 | volver | zurückkehren; zurückkommen | to come back | revenir |
| 1 | vosotros | ihr | ~~we~~ you | vous |
| 20 | vuelta por la ciudad, la | Stadtrundfahrt, die | to go for a walk in town | le tour en ville |

## Y

| UNIDAD | ESPAÑOL | ALEMÁN | INGLÉS | FRANCÉS |
|---|---|---|---|---|
| 1 | y | und | and | et |
| 10 | ya | schon | already; now | déjà |
| 5 | yerno, el | Schwiegersohn, der | son-in-law | le beau-fils |
| 2 | yugoslavo | jugoslawisch; Jugoslawe, der | Y(J)ugoslavian | Yougouslave |

## Z

| UNIDAD | ESPAÑOL | ALEMÁN | INGLÉS | FRANCÉS |
|---|---|---|---|---|
| 12 | zapatería, la | Schuhgeschäft, das | shoeshop | chez le cordonnièr |
| 12 | zapatilla, la | Hausschuh; Pantoffel, der | slipper | le chausson/la pantoufle |
| 4 | zapato, el | Schuh, der | shoe | la chaussure |
| 8 | zorro, el | Fuchs, der | fox | le renard |
| 12 | zueco, el | Holzschuh, der | clog | la galoche |
| 8 | zurcir | flicken | to mend | repriser |

# ÍNDICE DEL ESPAÑOL

| | | |
|---|---|---:|
| Letra | A | 3 |
| » | B | 8 |
| » | C | 10 |
| » | CH | 16 |
| » | D | 17 |
| » | E | 21 |
| » | F | 25 |
| » | G | 27 |
| » | H | 29 |
| » | I | 31 |
| » | J | 33 |
| » | K | 34 |
| » | L | 35 |
| » | LL | 37 |
| » | M | 38 |
| » | N | 41 |
| » | O | 43 |
| » | P | 45 |
| » | Q | 51 |
| » | R | 52 |
| » | S | 55 |
| » | T | 59 |
| » | U | 62 |
| » | V | 63 |
| » | Y | 65 |
| » | Z | 66 |